Settle & C

Country

Including a new long-distance walk and cycle route from Leeds to Carlisle

by

Colin Speakman

and

John Morrison

Series Editor, Stan Abbott

Settle & Carlisle Country

Published by Leading Edge Press and Publishing, the Old Chapel, Burtersett, Hawes, North Yorkshire, DL8 3PB.
☎ (0969) 667566

British Library Cataloguing in Publication Data

Speakman, Colin, *1941-*
    Settle and Carlisle Country: featuring a new long distance route for walkers and cyclists between Leeds and Carlisle. — (RailTrail Series)
    1. Northern England. Countryside adjacent to Settle and Carlisle
    I. Title II. Morrison, John, *1951-* III. Series
    796.51094278

    ISBN 0-948135-16-6

RailTrail Series editor, and designer: Stan Abbott

Sketch maps by Ruth Abbott, Barbara Drew and Alan Howard

Type: Leading Edge Press & Publishing

Colour reprographics: Impression, Leeds

Printed and bound in Great Britain by Ebenezer Baylis and Son Ltd, Worcester

RailTrail series logo by Barbara Drew

Contents

The sections of this book which cover the area between Leeds and Kirkby Stephen were written by Colin Speakman. Those covering the Eden Valley were written by John Morrison, who also wrote the text for the walk in Crummackdale. Additional material was contributed by Alan Howard, who wrote the Carlisle and Clitheroe trails.

Acknowledgements

Thanks for assistance in compiling this book go to Lydia Speakman, Helen Dias of the Eden Tourist Action Programme; Alice J Bondi of the East Cumbria Countryside Project; David Hanson, Vice Chairman of the Keighley and Worth Valley Railway; Brian Sutcliffe, Chairman of the Friends of the Settle and Carlisle Line; John Kevey of the Embsay Steam Railway; Ray Singleton, Rights of Way Officer at Cumbria County Council; Sue Arnott and Rae Lonsdale at the Yorkshire Dales National Park Authority; British Waterways Board; and British Rail and its friendly and courteous staff on the Settle-Carlisle line.

Maps

The maps which accompany the walks in this book are sketched for guidance only and are not to scale. The publishers strongly recommend that walkers also carry the relevant Ordance Survey sheet. The appropriate 1:50,000 series sheets are: nos. 85, 86, 90, 91, 98, 103, 104. The 1:25,000 scale map of the Yorkshire Dales is also recommended. On the Settle-Carlisle Way, the walkers' route is marked by dots, while the one for cyclists is shown by chevrons. The pictorial map on page 32 was drawn by Ruth Abbott.

We advise walkers to wear strong footwear, and carry waterproof clothing and provisions. A compass is also recommended, particularly on the upland sections. Observe the Country Code!

Foreword

NOT long after the Government's remarkable U-turn which led to the reprieve of the superb line from Settle to Carlisle, a conference was held in Leeds to bring together all those with an interest in building a prosperous new future for the railway.

Conspicuous among those present were representatives of ventures which had been involved in failed negotiations to turn the line into a tourism-led private enterprise.

The invitation to them at the conference was to bury their pride and work with British Rail and the local authorities.

Sadly, that is something which they have, by and large, failed to do.

We at Leading Edge Press and Publishing would like to think, however, that this book will, in its own small way, help redress the balance.

Along with our *Settle-Carlisle Express* newspaper, *Settle & Carlisle Country* aims to encourage use of the line by visitors to the area, thereby building on its importance as a transport artery for those of us who live and work near its route.

We hope that the Settle-Carlisle Way will become a popular route for walkers and a *de facto* Long Distance Path in much the same way as Wainwright's Coast to Coast Walk has become.

We commend it to you and wish you happy walking. And we thank British Rail's enthusiastic management for its support and enterprise in support of our ventures.

Stan Abbott, Publisher, Hawes, March 1990

Photography: All the "non-railway" pictures in this book were taken by John Morrison. The railway pictures were taken by Steve Batty, with the exception of the one on page 113, which is by John Sager.

This page: Farmhouse near Langwathby.
Facing page: No. 47465 passes Blea Moor Box with a Leicester-Edinburgh special.

Introduction

THERE is probably no other railway line in England which runs through such spectacular country as the Settle-Carlisle line. By rights it should never have been built, such were the engineering difficulties of constructing a line over the Pennine hills.

Despite the line's unique character, and the great engineering feat it represents, it was recently within a whisker of being closed down. That trains still ply this splendid line is due to the commitment of people who felt strongly that the line should not simply be allowed to die. So the railway represents a double triumph — celebrating both the navvies who laboured on tunnels and viaducts, and the pressure groups, MPs and local authorities who spoke up for the railway when all might have seemed lost. It makes an interesting story.

The beginnings of this Pennine railway arguably owe more to one man's frustration than to any grand strategy. James Allport was general manager of the Midland Railway Company back in the 1860s, when the railway company was trying to expand its operations from London to the North. The Midland ran trains as far north as Ingleton, just a few miles from Settle. However the track leading north from Ingleton belonged to a rival outfit, the London North Western Railway, and formed part of its Lancaster-Carlisle line.

Mr Allport's north-bound passengers had to disembark at Ingleton, and dash across the village to board a "connecting" LNWR train. But such was the low priority the LNWR gave to Midland travellers that all too often they would be greeted by the sight of their train disappearing into the distance. Nor would the LNWR allow Midland trains access to track from Ingleton to Edinburgh. The Midland company was losing passengers to its competitors; small wonder, then, that James Allport felt stymied.

Thus it was that the Midland began to

look for other solutions to the problem. What was needed was a new route to Carlisle, which would cut out the need to use LNWR trains at all. Railway engineers had already discounted the idea of a direct route to Carlisle, because of the hilly Pennine terrain; nevertheless the Midland placed a bill before parliament which put forward this very idea.

By the time the bill was passed, in 1866, the company was having second thoughts about the wisdom of the plan. The bill may even have been an audacious bluff by the Midland company to persuade the LNWR to adopt a more co-operative attitude. We may never know; but if it *was* a bluff then it proved to be an expensive one, because parliament eventually insisted that the line should indeed go ahead. So it was that a veritable army of navvies was assembled in 1869 to build this most improbable of railways.

It was hard slog all the way. Instead of following the easier course of the valley bottoms, the line took a more direct route. This was to provide a track suitable for 100mph express trains that would deliver northbound passengers to Scotland in the shortest time. It also meant, however, that extensive engineering works — viaducts and tunnels in particular— were needed to keep gradients acceptably shallow.

The enterprise was hit by extreme weather conditions and unforeseen engineering problems. The Settle-Carlisle railway was to prove more expensive — in every sense — than had ever been envisaged. The final cost in money was £3.5 million, instead of the projected £2 million. And the human price paid can be gauged from the memorial and the many gravestones at St Leonard's church in Chapel-le-Dale, commemorating the men who perished during the building of the railway.

All along the embryonic line there sprang up shanty towns, with colourful names such as Jericho, Sebastopol and Batty Wife. At Ribblehead alone more than 2,000 navvies lived in makeshift dwellings while they built the 24-arch viaduct. It must have been a wild and lawless place, like a scene from the American gold rush. Conditions were so insanitary that more than a hundred people succumbed to an outbreak of smallpox.

Technical problems were magnified by the uncompromising route through the dales. With speed of travel viewed as the highest priority, curves had to be gentle. To enable the gradient to be no more than one-in-100, there were to be a total of 325 bridges, 21 viaducts and 14 tunnels. Where hills were encountered, tunnels were bored through. Valleys were spanned by viaducts. Marshy ground was laboriously filled in, though at Dandry Mire, at the head of Garsdale, the peat bog soaked up as much material as the navvies tipped into it. Instead of the planned embankment, a ten-arch viaduct was finally built.

The line runs through some of the least inhabited areas of the country; nevertheless there were 19 stations built to serve the needs of the local community. But the fact that many stations — Dent and Kirkby Stephen, for example — are so distant from the townships whose names they bear only emphasises the line's status as a high-speed, all-weather route to the north.

It is no accident that the station buildings themselves bear a distinct "family resemblance". The Midland company used similar "Midland Gothic" designs, in small, medium and large sizes, for all the buildings on the Settle-Carlisle line. With their steeply pitched roofs and

Right: A limestone pavement typical of the Yorkshire Dales country traversed by the Settle-Carlisle line.

stone-faced walls (limestone in the Dales, red sandstone in the Eden valley section) they add a good deal of interest to the journey.

The line in its entirety took both passenger and freight traffic from St Pancras station in London, to Carlisle, and then on to Edinburgh and Glasgow. The Settle-Carlisle traverse is 72 miles long; it was declared open in 1876. It is good to know that despite all the attempts at closing it down, travellers of today can still take this most scenic of train journeys.

Rails through the fells

A DESCRIPTION OF THE LEEDS-CARLISE LINE

The total journey from Leeds to Carlisle — the area covered by this book — is 112 miles. The section of line between Leeds and Skipton could be described as "Metroland", now that there are more frequent services, thanks to the West Yorkshire Passenger Transport Authority (Metro), using new rolling stock and calling at a number of new and reopened stations. This section of the railway runs along the river Aire which — along with the construction of the Leeds-Liverpool canal more than two centuries ago — was largely responsible for the rise of Leeds as a heartland of textile and other industries.

As soon as you pull out of Leeds City station you can see the evidence of this history. The Aire valley combines a wealth of industrial remains with a surprisingly rural aspect, first of parks and later of open fields. For a few miles the river, railway and canal compete for space along the valley with a plethora of old textile mills.

Look out on your right for Kirkstall Abbey, one of the finest Cirstercian ruins in Europe. Thackley tunnel, encountered a few minutes later is, at 1,496 yards, the longest on the line until we reach the heart of the Yorkshire Dales. Shipley station derives its triangular shape from being a sort of railway "T-junction". Hardly has the train left Shipley than it makes a stop at Saltaire station — newly restored and reopened in 1984.

Saltaire is a delightful model village, built for his workforce by the paternalistic mill-owner Sir Titus Salt. Nearby is the huge mill itself, complete with its imposing facade and Italianesque campanile. It now belongs to the entrepreneur Jonathan Silver, who has converted the premises into a conference centre and gallery space. The 1853 Gallery now houses the country's biggest collection of works by Bradford-born artist, David Hockney.

A few miles further on, at Bingley, travellers will catch sight of the celebrated Five Rise Locks on the canal, which can raise or lower boats by sixty feet in the space of just a few yards. Only half a mile further is Crossflatts station, the only wholly new station to be opened in recent times.

Keighley Station keeps its status as a junction thanks to the Keighley and Worth Valley Railway. Passengers on this lovingly restored line can travel back in time on old steam trains — at weekends and main holiday times — to "Brontëland", otherwise known as Haworth. The stations on this line have also been restored, even down to the period advertising hoardings, and one, at Ingrow West, was rebuilt stone by stone from remains brought from Lancashire.

There is a new station at Cononley, one under construction at Steeton, and one at Cross Hills that is still at the planning stage. The local Metro trains terminate at Skipton, while through trains go on to either Morecambe or Carlisle.

Nearby is the Embsay Steam Railway, another fascinating restored line. Though the round trip is only four miles at the time of writing, plans are well

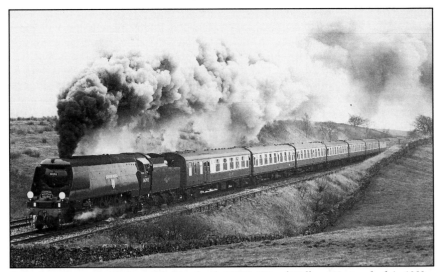

Steam is now a regular feature of the line: here's 34092, City of Wells, at Horton, back in 1983, when the future of the line was much less certain.

well advanced to relay track to the ever-popular beauty spot of Bolton Abbey.

Skipton calls itself the Gateway to the Dales, and with good reason. With its broad main street leading away from the well-preserved castle, this bustling town has kept its medieval layout with alleyways and courtyards leading off the market place. In Skipton are the last mills that travellers see until the train pulls into Carlisle.

The line parts company with the River Aire at Gargrave; at Hellifield it joins both the River Ribble and the old Lancashire and Yorkshire railway from Blackburn and Clitheroe. Hellifield used to be a more important junction than it is now, which explains the presence of the elaborate station building with its ornamental canopies. It looks rather neglected now, though there are hopes it may one day be restored to its former Victorian splendour.

Another characteristic sight all along the line are the railwaymens' cottages. Generally arranged in short terraces, and recognisably in the same architectural style as the stations, they are sel-

dom more than a stone's throw from the line.

The railway heads northwards, hugging the Ribble, until Settle Junction is reached; from here the line to Carnforth bears off. Settle Junction is the start of 22 miles of continuous uphill gradient, dubbed "the long drag" by the footplatemen who laboured to maintain a full head of steam to complete the ascent.

This is limestone country, and Settle is dwarfed by the limestone cliffs of Giggleswick Scar which are part of the Craven Fault. The line passes a number of limestone quarries; all are ugly blots on the Dales landscape. At one time the trains carried away the stone, used in the road-making and construction industries. Now these loads are carried by lorries, with all the traffic pollution that results.

In the search for high ground the line runs through the centre of Settle, and over the main road on a viaduct. This busy little town also marks the southern boundary of the Yorkshire Dales National Park, with its rolling hills and valleys. Yet the route taken by the train follows the River Ribble and takes in some very bleak fells indeed. Bleak they may be, yet they are not lacking in interesting features. Look out for the unmistakable profile of Pen y Ghent — one of the famous "three peaks" — on the right as you approach Horton-in-Ribblesdale.

The second peak — Ingleborough — soon looms up on the left. Then you will see Ribblehead viaduct, perhaps the finest example of railway engineering on the whole line and, ironically, the edifice which was the scapegoat for the line's near demise. It was the alleged cost of renovating or replacing the viaduct (a scheduled Ancient Monument) which fuelled the proposals for closing the route.

The Ribblehead viaduct's 24 arches, the tallest 100 feet high, seem to be in tune with their bleak moorland surroundings, with the featureless mass of Whernside, the third of the three peaks, as a backdrop. This is a favourite spot for photographers hoping to capture the archetypal image of a train under steam. They generally have time to fire off a few frames, as trains have to slow down for the single-track crossing of the viaduct.

Northbound travellers will barely notice Ribblehead station, since it is only southbound trains which stop there now. However, the reinstatement of the other platform is a fairly high priority since the line's salvation. The nearby Station Inn, incongruously sited in this bleak landscape, is a reminder of the days when the road here was an important stagecoach route.

Across the inhospitable expanse of Blea Moor, and past a remote (but still active) signal box, the line plunges into Blea Moor tunnel: the longest on the line at 2,629 yards as well as the deepest (500ft). The train emerges into daylight to give a panoramic view of Dentdale, a welcome sight after the bleakness of the moors. The line follows a spectacular "shelf" along the fellside, crossing Dent Head and Artengill viaducts.

Enjoy the views down Dentdale and the rounded Howgill Hills beyond, before arriving at Dent station which, at 1,100 feet above sea level, is the highest on a main line in England. Snow fences in the vicinity attest to hard winters of the past when trains were occasionally buried by snow-drifts.

The village of Dent is a good four miles from the station. However the walk from the station takes in some superb riverside scenery, and Dent itself — with its whitewashed houses and cobbled streets — is a delight.

The train travels through the Rise Hill tunnel, to emerge in Garsdale, a few miles from the station. The old Wensleydale line used to branch off here, but the last remaining passenger section — to Hawes — was closed in 1959.

Garsdale has proved to be one of the most popular of the reopened stations because it is mid-way between Hawes and Sedbergh — both towns popular with visitors — and a minibus service connects with many of the train arrivals. Here, too, there was once a turntable which had to be surrounded by fencing after a train began to spin round uncontrollably in the teeth of a gale. It was only brought to a standstill by tipping sand into the turntable pit. The pit remains, but the turntable itself has been removed to Keighley station.

From Garsdale, the line crosses Dandry Mire viaduct, and negotiates three short tunnels, to emerge at Aisgill — at 1,169ft this is both the summit of the line and the source of the river Eden. These bleak and seldom-visited fells are known as Mallerstang. Here we leave Yorkshire, and its dales, as the train crosses into Cumbria. We also join the more pastoral valley of the Eden, one of the few English rivers to flow northwards. We stay with this river much of the way to Carlisle.

No. 47587 hauls the 07.50 Manchester-Glasgow across Artengill Viaduct on 6 April 1985; since then, traffic on the line has risen considerably.

On the right, in the valley bottom, is the ruin of Pendragon castle, reputedly the birthplace of King Arthur. On to Kirkby Stephen station, actually more than a mile from the town itself because of the need to maintain a gentle gradient on the line. The landscape, too, is gentler here, as the line crosses Smardale viaduct, the highest on the route and the last in limestone country.

The village of Crosby Garrett is bisected by a red sandstone viaduct. As we enter the broad plain of the lower Eden valley, we are at the half-way point between Settle and Carlisle. The line crosses the Eden for the first time on the 90ft high Ormside viaduct, and brings us to Appleby. Until Westmorland was absorbed into Cumbria in 1974, Appleby was the county town.

It is a handsome and historic town, with a fine Norman castle, a tree-lined main street and two medieval churches. In June every year the famous horse-fairs are held here. The town also has the only manned station on the line between Settle and Carlisle.

North of Appleby there are fine views,

to the right, of the Pennine hills — including Cross Fell, the highest at 2,930ft — while to the left, in the distance, are the more sharply delineated peaks of the Lake District. The topography of this area is sometimes responsible for producing dramatic air turbulence, known as the Helm wind. In the days when steam trains ran daily, and not just on special excursions, the Helm was reputed to have broken carriage windows and even to have whisked the coal off the firemens' shovels.

From Langwathby to Lazonby the line follows a particularly beautiful stretch of the Eden valley, where the river has cut an impressive wooded gorge through the red sandstone. The scenery here is reminiscent of the highlands of Scotland.

To maintain a straight route, the line then leaves the valley bottom and negotiates a number of tunnels, cuttings and embankments before crossing the 80ft high viaduct at Coombe Eden. From the station at Armathwaite you can look down to the right and see the village and fortified hall below.

river has cut an impressive wooded gorge through the red sandstone. The scenery here is reminiscent of the highlands of Scotland.

To maintain a straight route, the line then leaves the valley bottom and negotiates a number of tunnels, cuttings and embankments before crossing the 80ft high viaduct at Coombe Eden. From the station at Armathwaite you can look down to the right and see the village and fortified hall below.

After Armathwaite the line escorts the river once again until the disused station at Cotehill is reached; from here the railway strikes west on the last leg to Carlisle. The line joins the Newcastle-Carlisle railway (almost 40 years older than the Settle-Carlisle line) a couple of miles from the city's Citadel station. This magnificent structure recalls the days when this was a joint operation involving no fewer than eight railway companies, each with its own yards and engine shed. Even the station's refreshment room is built in a mock medieval style.

Don't simply cross over the platform and take the first train back down the line; Carlisle is well worth taking time to explore. The remains of the citadel, from which the station gets its name, now comprise a pair of sturdy sandstone towers — built as a second line of defence against marauding Scots. The *first* line of defence of this border city was another splendid feat of engineering: Hadrian's Wall. Carlisle also held out stoutly against aggressors from the south, remaining unconquered for a full 26 years after the Norman invasion of 1066.

The way ahead

The Settle-Carlisle line has been called "the line that should never have been built". It nearly became known as "the line that died", and if that decision had been left solely in the hands of British Rail, this book would be merely another exercise in nostalgia, yet more yearning for what we fondly imagine were the "good old days".

That trains still run at all is due to the fact that enough people decided to stand up to the powers that be and let their feelings be known. Railways in general tend to attract strong feelings, and the Settle-Carlisle line has a particular place in the affections of those whose hearts beat faster at the sound of a train whistle. This is no ordinary railway line, as British Rail discovered when it initiated a policy dubbed by its critics as "closure by stealth": that is, hoping that if the line were closed down gradually, with a minimum of fuss, then perhaps no-one would notice.

When the line opened, in 1876, there were three express trains daily going each way from London to Edinburgh and Glasgow. The busiest era was the beginning of the century, and we can trace the decline of the Settle-Carlisle railway to a date as early as the first world war. Wartime cuts in services were followed by the amalgamation of many railway companies in 1923 — including those old rivals, the LNWR and the Midland, which both became part of the London, Midland and Scottish Railway.

After the second world war a succession of closures was begun which continued into the 1970s. The Wensleydale line, which connected at Garsdale, became a casualty. In 1960 the same fate befell the Kirkby Stephen-Tebay line. Other "feeder" lines or passenger services gradually disappeared, such as that from Blackburn to Hellifield.

On the Settle-Carlisle route itself, the stations began to close: Scotby in 1942; Cotehill, Ormside and Crosby Garrett a decade later; Cumwhinton in 1956. Many other stations were gradually downgraded to the status of unmanned halts.

Ribblehead viaduct under construction in about 1873 — note the wooden scaffolding. Part of the Batty Green shanty town can just be seen in the background.

As pressure groups were beginning to find their voices, local train services were ended in 1970. Another clutch of stations became no more than blurs glimpsed by travellers as they sped by. Horton, Ribblehead, Dent, Garsdale, Kirkby Stephen, Long Marton, Newbiggin, Culgaith, Langwathby, Little Salkeld, Lazonby and Kirkoswald, and Armathwaite: all were closed. This left Settle and Appleby as the only intermediate stations. Some station buildings were sold to private buyers, others gradually fell into a state of disrepair.

This was more or less the state of play as we came into the 1980s. With BR cutting services and amenities to the bone, the closure of the whole Settle-Carlisle line seemed to be coming sooner rather than later. By 1982, through freight trains were being diverted away from the line.

A year later came the crunch: the formal notice of closure. If British Rail thought it had quietly achieved its objective, then it had badly underestimated the howl of protest that its action would provoke.

Ironically, it was the prospect of closure which brought many paying travellers to use the Settle-Carlisle line for the first time. How often do we fail to

value things until they are about to disappear! However, having travelled the line once — perhaps just to see what all the fuss was about — many people came back again and again. In 1981 an association was formed: the Friends of the Settle-Carlisle Line. This organisation, in tandem with other interested bodies, gave a unified voice to all those who protested about the closure plans, and proved in time to be very effective at lobbying British Rail.

It had actually been a few years earlier, in 1974, that the DalesRail idea was born, when a quartet of fell-walkers were bemoaning British Rail's attitude to their rural lines. The idea was for the Ramblers' Association to charter a train over the Settle-Carlisle line, and to reopen — temporarily at least — some of the closed stations. Permission was obtained from BR, the Ramblers' Association agreed to put up the money, and this one-off trip went ahead. It proved to be a remarkable success, with a total of 500 walkers enjoying a day out in the Dales.

By the following year this one-off excursion had become a genuine railway service, which took walkers deep into the Dales national park, provided minibus links, and even guided walks. A three-year experiment was, in 1977, reckoned to have been a great success; the DalesRail scheme was even being praised by the British Tourist Authority.

By this time, many people were involved in the project, such as the Yorkshire Dales National Park (which acquired new powers in 1974), local authorities and even a new group of enthusiasts banded under the title of Friends of DalesRail. The Settle-Carlisle line was beginning to look like an amenity that people cared about, instead of just a railway line deemed surplus to requirements.

Yet the line itself had not been adequately maintained. It seems that British Rail had had closure in mind for many years, because it had allowed many structures such as viaducts to be neglected. Ribblehead viaduct, for example, was cited as needing replacement at a cost of about £6m. Other voices insisted that this figure had been deliberately inflated.

The state of the line at the time of writing is remarkably healthy, considering that the patient was considered not long ago to be a terminal case. The threat of closure has been lifted. Passengers numbers are up (around 500,000 in 1989), regular train services are being maintained and expanded, and steam — in the shape of special excursion trains — is a regular feature on the line. With the closure threat lifted, an enthusiastic BR management — often in co-operation with user groups — appears committed to the success of the improved services. In short, the future of the Settle-Carlisle line can now be debated rationally, without worrying about imminent closure.

One thing is certain: if we want this fascinating railway to survive into the next millenium, then we have to use it. This book combines trips on the railway with some excellent walks. The main walk which accompanies the line all the way from Leeds to Carlisle — and the cycle route that begins at Skipton — do not stick slavishly to the railway itself, but are designed to take in particularly good terrain and a host of interesting features on the way. Some of these features will appeal to lovers of railway history, while others, such as ancient remains, old buildings and beautiful landscapes, are of more general interest.

The main walk is divided up into manageable chunk, each chunk being a day's walk for an experienced walker. At the end of each day, walkers will arrive at a railway station and, in most instances, a nearby village or town with overnight accommodation. Some walkers will think of the whole 150-mile route as a long-distance walk, to be completed in one go. Most walkers, however — and especially families with young children — will prefer to treat each day's section as a walk in its own right, and use the train to return to the station from which each walk commenced. A train journey — however short — can be a satisfying way to end a day's walk.

In addition to the main route there are a number of circular rambles, for which stations provide both the starting and finishing points. Enjoy the walks, however you decide to use this book, and be sure to remember the ingenuity — perhaps even the bloody-mindedness — of our Victorian forebears who managed to build this remarkable railway through the Pennine hills. ❏

The railway from Leeds to Carlisle, with the S & C Way marked in red. The stations marked with white dots are planned to be reopened.

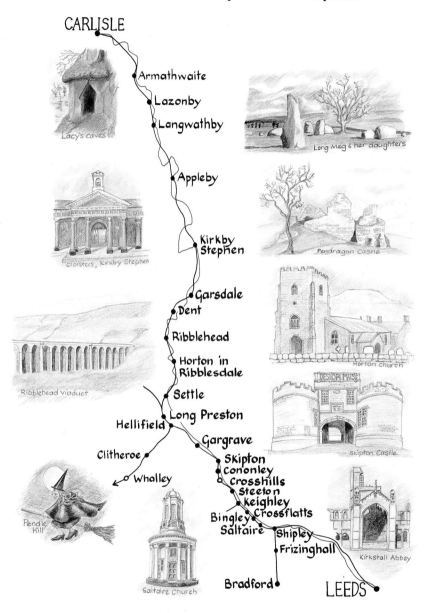

Leeds to Saltaire

*A 14-mile (25km) walk from the
industrial heartland of West Yorkshire,
along the towpath of the Leeds-Liverpool
Canal, to a fascinating "model" village.*

LEEDS is one of Britain's greatest cities, with a population of more than three quarters of a million, and is now the major administrative and financial centre of West Yorkshire and the wider Yorkshire and Humberside region. The city is also a major cultural centre, with the West Yorkshire Playhouse, Opera North, the City Museum and Art Gallery, the Henry Moore Sculpture Gallery and much more besides.

Yet Leeds is a relatively new city. In medieval days it was little more than a hamlet in the ancient forest of Elmet, at a time when Rothwell — now little more than a suburb — was the more significent settlement. Leeds grew to prominence, however, as the wool textile industries developed in the Pennines in Tudor times, powered by the waters of fast-flowing streams.

Leeds, being the highest navigable point on the River Aire, became a principal trading centre for textiles. Buying and selling took place on Leeds Bridge itself (close to the start of the Settle-Carlisle Way) before moving to two purpose-built cloth halls: the White Cloth Hall and the Coloured Cloth Hall. White Cloth Hall is commemorated by the name of one of the principal roads from the west leading into the city — Whitehall Road — while the facade and part of the structure of the Coloured Cloth Hall survives between the Corn Exchange and the railway line.

In later years, Leeds became famous for the manufacture of clothing and for heavy engineering — particularily the building of traction engines and railway locomotives. Firms such as Kitson's, Fowler's and the Hunslet Engine Company (currently making locomotives for the Channel Tunnel) became known throughout the world.

Other household names associated with Leeds are Burton's ("Top Shop"), Hepworth's ("Next") and Marks and Spencers, who first opened their "Penny Bazaar" in the city's handsome Victorian market.

You can see much of Leeds' early history illustrated in the excellent Armley Mills Industrial Museum, which is passed on the Leeds-Settle-Carlisle Way.

Much of the Victorian city survives: the magnificent Town Hall, dating from the 1850s and a symbol of municipal pride (although the city's administration has moved to the Civic Hall), the recently restored Corn Exchange, the market, and some splendid pedestrianised shopping streets and arcades. (Leeds was, in fact, the first city in the UK to introduce extensive pedestrianisation of its central streets.) But there are some impressive new developments too, particularily south of the River Aire. New shops, offices and houses reflect the city's increasing prosperity as a financial and administrative centre.

The Settle-Carlisle Way begins outside City Station and City Square with its famous statue of the Black Prince. Turn right in front of Queen's Hotel to Bishopgate traffic lights, then right again down Bishopgate, going underneath the "Dark Arches" below the station.

As you get to the bottom end of the broad tunnel, turn right into the "Arches Arcade", signed to the Canal Basin. Walk between impressive tall brick arches and a series of subterranean bridges over the River Aire into an area of shops and arcades — Granary Wharf — before turning left into Leeds Canal Basin.

Waterways first made Leeds important, and the city is still an inland port on the Aire and Calder Navigation. (A "Navigation" is a hybrid between a navigable river and a canal, containing stretches of "improved" river and lengths of more orthodox canal with lock gates to avoid difficult or circuitous stretches). Boats can still travel as far as Goole or Hull on the Humber, or into the Ouse or Trent river systems.

The Leeds Canal Basin is where the 127-mile Leeds-Liverpool Canal begins its cross-Pennine journey, locking in from the Aire and Calder system. But unlike the Aire and Calder, the Leeds-Liverpool is no longer a commercial waterway. It is one of the many canals still maintained by

British Waterways Board for leisure uses — recreational boating and cruising, angling, and walking, and as an important source of industrial water supply.

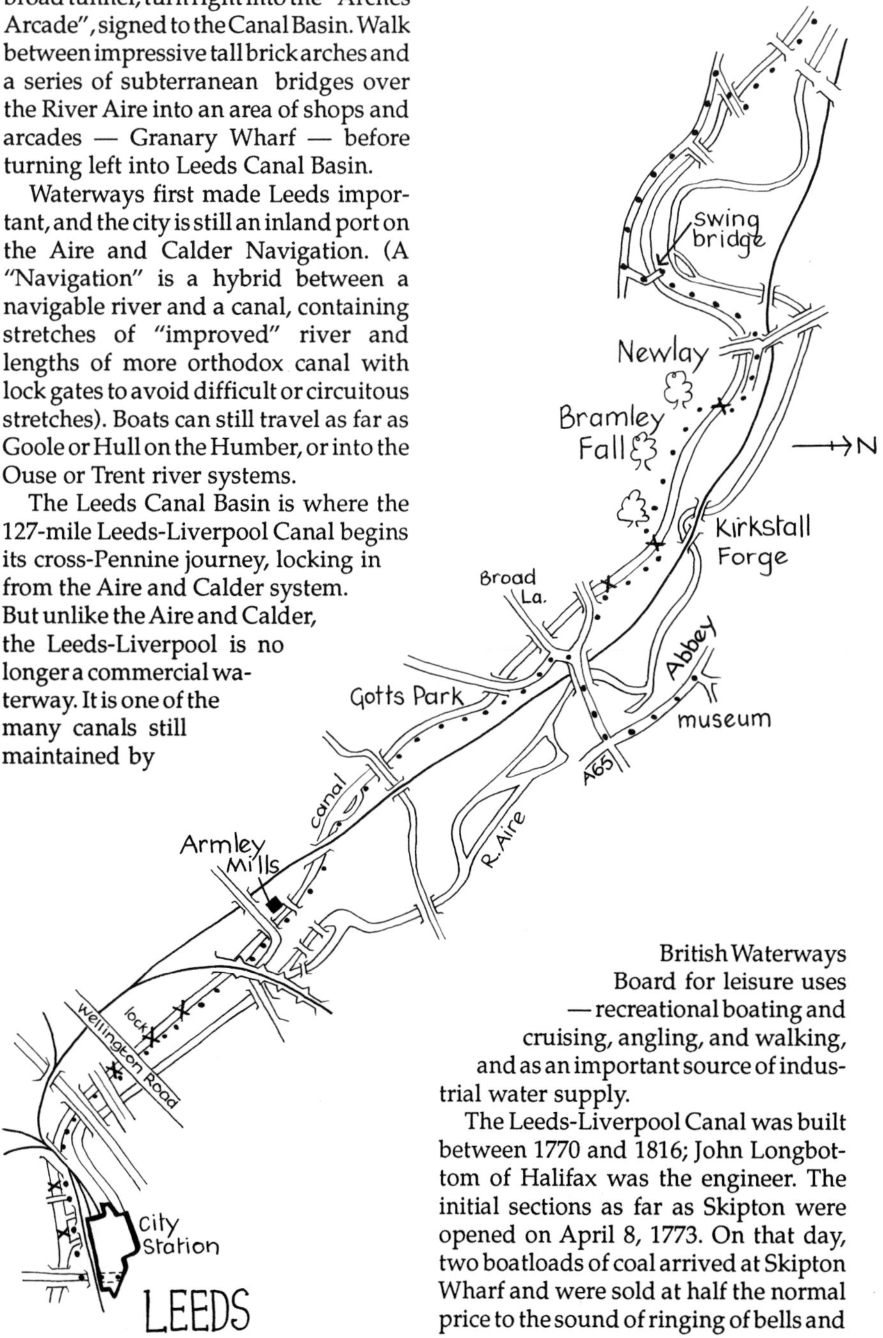

The Leeds-Liverpool Canal was built between 1770 and 1816; John Longbottom of Halifax was the engineer. The initial sections as far as Skipton were opened on April 8, 1773. On that day, two boatloads of coal arrived at Skipton Wharf and were sold at half the normal price to the sound of ringing of bells and

swing bridge

Newlay

Bramley Fall

Kirkstall Forge

Broad La.

→N

Abbey

museum

Gotts Park

A65

canal

R. Aire

Armley Mills

Wellington Road

lock

City Station

LEEDS

19

Opposite: The imposing facade of Kirkstall Abbey sits on a grassy site just a couple of miles from the centre of Leeds.
Top: Arched doorways and windows are distinctive features of Saltaire — the model village built by SirTitus Salt to house the workers at his massive textile mill.
Bottom: One of the best-known features on the Leeds-Liverpool canal is the spectacular cascade of Five Rise Locks at Bingley.

Armley Mills Industrial Museum and the towpath of the Leeds-Liverpool canal.

by the light of bonfires. Four years later the route was opened as far as Gargrave, to transport lead from the Duke of Devonshire's mines on Grassington Moor.

However, economic recession and the Napoleonic Wars caused abandonment of the construction until funds were available. It was 39 years later before a flotilla of gaily decorated boats could make the full trip from Leeds to Liverpool.

The building of the canal had a profound impact on the Aire valley. It provided cheap raw materials — most notably coal, iron, limestone and raw wool — and allowed finished goods to be exported in considerable quantities to world markets.

Little wonder that the canal still links countless mills which originated in the latter years of the 18th or early 19th centuries. It is a "contour" canal in that it exploits the natural topography of the valley, sharing it with the River Aire, the

former turnpike roads, the railway and modern by-passes. It can also be termed a "broad" canal, with wider locks than the later, more heavily engineered "narrow" canals.

It is still the only canal open across the Pennines, for cruise if not commercial traffic, as one of British Waterways Board's Leisure Waterways. There are, however, plans afoot to reopen both the Rochdale and the Huddersfield canals.

Much of the Leeds-Liverpool Canal goes through a green corridor of semi-natural or regenerated countryside, making it a magnificent linear park and natural walkway, as rich in natural history as industrial archaeology.

Note, for example, the original Regency period canal transhipment warehouse, with cast iron columns, on the far side of the canal basin. At least one fine old dockside crane remains, though no longer in use. You will see many examples of original machinery and equipment, perhaps renewed and modernised but still performing the same function.

Turn right alongside the car exit road towards the little Georgian canal office and the first locks on the Leeds-Liverpool Canal before bearing right, alongside the railway wall, onto the canal towpath.

The first six miles of the Leeds-Liverpool Canal towpath have been designated the Museum of Leeds Trail, in recognition of the architectural and industrial heritage both of the canal and of the whole Kirkstall valley. A leaflet available from the City Museum in the Headrow, or from Armley Mills Industrial Museum, gives a detailed, illustrated account of the many features that make the canalside so important and interesting.

This is easy, level walking with no wayfinding problems. Things to note include fine views across the River Aire and the changing skyline of the city. Tall office blocks and semi-skyscrapers compete with the old church towers and the distinctive white clock tower of the University's Parkinson Building. Look out on the right for the remarkable Tower Works with its twin red-brick campaniles — actually factory chimneys, but brilliant copies of bell-towers to be found in Verona and Florence.

You soon go underneath Monk Bridge which carries Whitehall Road and the even more elegant Leeds and Thirsk Railway bridge of 1846. Until the 1960s this was used by streamlined "A4" steam pacifics hauling crack expresses such as *The White Rose Pullman* to London King's Cross from the now vanished Leeds Central Station.

Continue under the modern and uninspiring concrete Wellington Road bridge, past the splendid 1838 Castleton Mill with its handsome bay windows. Climb up Spring Garden Locks, with their lovely lock-keepers' cottages. There are good views from here over the river,

back to the city, and across the Victorian suburbs of Burley and Woodhouse.

Shortly to be seen on the left is the site of a Norman motte and bailey castle at Giant's Hill. Then comes the old Leeds Forge, and the impressive Leeds-Thirsk Railway viaduct, built in 1846 to carry the old line to the north from Leeds across the Aire valley. It is still in use as far as Harrogate, and is now the Metro-Train Harrogate line to Burley Park, Headingley and Horsforth.

To view the Industrial Museum in Armley Mills, leave the towpath at Canal Road by the steps and follow the drive to the museum entrance along the south side of the canal.

There have been corn and fulling mills on this site since the 16th century, utilising the natural water-power of the river and its falls. Most of the present mill dates from 1804-5 when it was the largest and most advanced in the whole of Europe.

In the museum there are waterwheels, a rare fulling mill, and exhibitions of tanning, weaving, cloth-making and tailoring. You can also see a variety of locomotives, engines and cranes, a recreated street of Jewish immigrant tailors, a restored thirties cinema, as well as much other material of interest. It is, in short, well worth the detour.

Your path continues along the towpath, soon going underneath the ironwork of the bridge that carries the Leeds-Settle-Carlisle railway. At this point the railway was once four-track, with a complex bridge. Near here, too, is a special bay arm of the canal, which was once used by barges to carry coal from the Yorkshire mines to Kirkstall Power Station. This is now demolished; only a complex of National Grid substations and pylon gantries survive.

A stone bridge, carrying Redcoat Lane into Gott's Park, soon crosses the canal. Keep ahead as the valley opens out in impressive style. The neo-classical house

Opposite: *Skipton is a bustling market town, but there are still some tranquil corners, such as this spur of the Leeds-Liverpool canal.*
Top: *Langcliffe, near Settle, is a typical Dales village, with attractive stone cottages and farm buildings huddled around a village green.*
Bottom: *The Dales section of the Settle-Carlisle Way goes through limestone country. These limekilns were used by farmers to produce lime to fertilise the land.*

on the hill in the parkland to the left is Armley House, which early last century was the home of Benjamin Gott, the great Leeds merchant and industrialist. Gott also had the park laid out by Humphrey Repton, the foremost landscape architect of his day, with elegant woods and pleasant vistas. It is still known as Gott's Park today, and is one of many well-kept urban parks of which Leeds is justly proud.

Keep ahead to Kirkstall Bridge and Bridge Road—a point known as "Amen Corner", reputedly because it was where the monks could be heard concluding their vespers!

For Kirkstall Abbey and the Abbey House Museum leave the canal towpath at the triangle of grass and benches at Bridge Road, and turn right. Continue to the traffic lights and turn left along the A65 to the Abbey (15 minutes walk). Frequent bus services run from here back to City Square.

Smoke-blackened Kirkstall Abbey is a landmark familiar to both rail passengers and towpath walkers. It is one of the finest early Cistercian ruins in the British Isles, and was founded in 1152 as a daughter house of Fountains Abbey. After the Dissolution in 1539 it was greatly neglected and became a fashionably romantic ruin — visited and painted by Turner and other artists.

It is now carefully preserved, and the nearby Abbey House Museum — in the original gatehouse of the Abbey — has a variety of toys, domestic items and restored streets and shops. There is also a remarkable Geological Garden with an outline map of the British Isles with typical rocks in correct geographical positions.

Return to the Way. Near the bridge, on Broad Lane, is Hollybush Farm; it was built in the last century, though the barn dates to the 1600s. The farm is now the regional centre for the British Trust for Conservation Volunteers who have

a tree nursery on the site. The huge building on the right, with small windows, is the former Kirkstall Brewery, built in the 1830s. Fine Yorkshire beers found their way from here by canal and steamships to places as far away as Australia and New Zealand.

Your path goes under the Leeds-Bradford turnpike road bridge and past low-lying fields, where rhubarb — a Yorkshire speciality, allegedly thriving in damp and soot — was once extensively grown. You pass Kirkstall Lock and reach Kirkstall Forge, an industrial complex which dates from the 17th century. It still contains its 17th and 18th century water-powered tilt hammers. These are not on public display, however, as the site is still busy with heavy engineering work. The forge is, in fact, one of the oldest sites in the world in continuous industrial use.

An area of lovely woodland — oak and birch — extends on the left. Bramley Fall Woods covered the site of extensive quarries, from which the famous West Riding millstone grit was exported all over the country. This stone was particularly valued in the building and engineering trades for its hard-wearing properties. It was used, for example, in the balustrades of London Bridge as well as for countless other bridges, docks and wharfs. If you want to explore the woods, leave the towpath by the footbridge at the lock and follow the path through the woods at the far side, rejoining the towpath at Newlay Locks.

Newlay Bridge, one of the oldest surviving iron bridges in the country, is well worth seeing. To reach it, take the footpath which bears right 200 yards past Newlay Locks, to Abbey Inn. Turn right here to reach the Bridge.

Continue along the towpath as the canal meanders over the next mile and a half to Rodley — a typical stone-built West Riding village which, like so many parts of Leeds, keeps its special identity within the overall city area. Many of Rodley's older houses back onto the canal, and the canal basin is now a busy marina which is generally crammed with a variety of small craft. If you are thirsty you can enjoy a drink at a canalside pub, the Rodley Barge.

Cross the swing bridge to Rodley village centre. From Rodley the canal towpath takes in a particularly beautiful stretch of Airedale, with river, canal and railway bending round in a beautiful green arch to Apperley Bridge.

The original Apperley Bridge is not the one across the River Aire which now carries the busy A658 road from Bradford to Harrogate. It was actually the older 18th century stone bridge some 50 yards further west. There is a fine old coaching inn nearby.

The towpath now swings northwards past more locks and underneath the railway as it heads into Thackley Tunnel. You follow another long loop, this time past Esholt with its large sewage works. Until relatively recently the works had their own internal railway system with a specially adapted steam locomotive powered by the oil from waste wool from Airedale Mills. The engine is now kept in Bradford Industrial Museum at Moorside Road, Greengate — just a few minutes walk from Apperley Bridge.

In medieval times, Esholt was the site of a nunnery. Now it is more famous as one of the settings used for Yorkshire Television's long-running soap opera Emmerdale Farm, and countless coach parties from all over Britain come to seek the original Woolpack Inn.

River and canal now curve westwards, soon to rejoin the railway as it emerges from the tunnel. The Bradford-

Top: The tranquil village of Dent has a split personality; it lies both within the county of Cumbria and the borders of the Yorkshire Dales National Park. In character, however, its cobbled streets and whitewashed houses seem to belong more to the Lake District.
Bottom: Wild Boar Fell recalls the days when wild boars were hunted in this area: the bleak yet beautiful valley of Mallerstang. Walkers on the Settle-Carlisle Way share the valley with both the railway and the infant River Eden.

Top: *Kirkby Stephen is a handsome market town that used to be a welcome stop for stagecoach travellers; at one time there were no fewer than 17 pubs! These distinctive cloisters, in front of the parish church, were once the site of the town's butter market.*
Bottom: *One of the highlights of the Settle-Carlisle Way is the riverside walk from Great Ormside into the historic town of Appleby. Here the tranquil waters of the River Eden meander through woodland and pasture.*

Ilkley branch comes in from the north, in a narrow neck of the valley at Shipley.

The canal basin here was where the long-vanished Bradford branch left the trunk route. The spur into Bradford, opened in 1774, had a chequered history. It became notoriously polluted with industrial waste and sewage, and was closed by Court Order in 1867. It was partially reopened in 1872, mainly to carry stone from Bolton Woods quarries, but was completely closed down in 1922. You can still trace the route it took, and its name survives in Canal Road which leads, as the canal itself did, into Bradford city centre.

An elegant footbridge over the canal leads to the main Leeds road. The tall buildings close by were once bargemens' lodgings. A short walk away, up the station drive, is Shipley's railway station. It was built in an unusual triangular formation, and is the only small station in West Yorkshire which still has four working platforms. One of them was built relatively recently to save trains on the main line having to reverse to stop at Shipley.

Many original Midland Railway features, both external and internal, survive in this building, and richly merit preservation as part of West Yorkshire's rail heritage. Shipley town itself is built around a modern market place, set back from the busy main roads, but there is a fine Victorian church to explore.

Continue along the towpath; on your left is Shipley Wharf, home of Apollo Canal Carriers. They operate a Water Bus service — with beautifully restored boats — between here and Bingley on summer Sundays, and put on both lunchtime and popular evening "starlight" dinner cruises.

This first stage of the Settle-Carlisle Way ends at Saltaire, which is easily reached past a group of canal cottages. You can wander into Saltaire's "Little Venice", a huge man-made canyon between vast mill walls. At the far side of Saltaire Bridge a walkway leads either to the footbridge over the parallel River Aire into Robert's Park or into the centre of Saltaire, with its handsome buildings around the broad main street of Victoria Road.

Developed during the 1850s, Sir Titus Salt's remarkable "model" mill village of Saltaire was built in a green and pleasant part of Airedale, to take his factory and workforce away from the slums and pollution of inner Bradford. He built the great mill close by, with a handsome Venetian campanile-style chimney.

At the peak of production the mill held 1,200 looms capable of weaving 30,000 yards of cloth every day, and more than 3,000 people were employed there. But he also developed a village for his employees which catered for their spiritual as well as material needs. There is an elegant Congregational Church, a town hall (whose lions are said to have been destined for Trafalgar Square, but rejected because they were too small), a school, a Mechanics' Institute, almshouses for retired workers, a riverside park, in which swearing and gambling were forbidden, but no pub!

An imposing statue of Sir Titus stands in the park, just visible from the towpath. He shares the podium with a llama and an alpaca (types of long-haired South American goat), whose fleeces helped to make his fortune.

The little boathouse by the river is now a "Victorian" restaurant and coffee shop. Visitors can enjoy the atmosphere of a typical Victorian tea-parlour, complete with harmonium of the period, or take a boat on the river. Close by can also be found the Victorian Reed Organ Museum, and the Shipley Glen Tramway — Britain's only inland rope-hauled funicular railway — is but a short walk away. A more detailed exploration of this fascinating area is to be found on page 104.

The canal basin at Rodley is a popular spot in summer for those who enjoy messing about in boats.

Saltaire station, in the centre of the village, has been beautifully restored by Metro — the Passenger Transport Authority — in period style. There are frequent MetroTrains on the Airedale line from here to Leeds, Bradford and Skipton. ❏

Top: Apart from the famous horse fair, held in June each year, Appleby is a quiet market town that still largely keeps its medieval layout. The main street runs from the Norman castle down to the parish church, cloisters and market cross.
Bottom: Just north of Langwathby are Long Meg and her Daughters, reckoned to be the second largest Neolithic stone circle in the country. While the purpose of the stones is unclear, their alignment does suggest a solar calendar.

Saltaire to Skipton

A 16-mile (26km) walk that reveals many aspects of the canal, and the villages alongside it, before you arrive in The Gateway to the Dales.

THIS section of the route continues through Airedale and still uses the towpath of the Leeds-Liverpool Canal. It contains some of the most beautiful and characteristic parts of this rather neglected area of Yorkshire, increasingly more rural in setting than the initial section from Leeds.

From Saltaire, the towpath follows an elevated section of waterway, with good views across Robert's Park (look out for the statue of Sir Titus Salt) and Salt's cricket ground.

Hirst Lock is soon reached; now follows one of the most delightful short stretches of the entire waterway, as the canal goes through an area of dense oak woods. Hirst Woods are rich in natural history, birdlife in particular; if you are lucky you may even catch sight of a kingfisher near the water. There is a prehistoric stone circle on the edge of the woods and a network of footpaths to explore.

Immediately beyond the woods, the canal crosses Dowley Gap Aqueduct, a magnificent eight-arch stone edifice which spans the river in fine style. There are good views along the valley as you cross. Shortly before the next locks, at Dowley Gap, the towpath crosses to the left side of the canal, over a bridge designed to cope with the horses' towing ropes. There is another canalside pub here, the Fisherman.

The canal makes its way into the narrowing gorge of the valley that contains Bingley. It's an impressive landscape of old mills, warehouses and wharfs. You emerge by the car-park and Waterbus stop just behind Bingley railway station.

Bingley is a delightful place to explore. Despite many industrial changes, this ancient Airedale town still keeps much of its character — particularly around the early Tudor church with its fine window designed by the pre-Raphaelite painter, Burne-Jones. The 17th century White Horse Inn is situated on what was Bingley's main street until its course was diverted through the churchyard early this century to cope with an increase in traffic.

Buried in the churchyard is John Nicholson (1790-1843), the Airedale poet: a perhaps unjustly neglected writer who drowned in the river Aire while returning home from a drinking spree in a local pub.

Myrtle Park is a fine Victorian park with attractive formal gardens and a small aviary. It extends almost into the town centre and then back to the river Aire. Riverside paths and a footbridge lead to the historic Beckfoot packhorse bridge on an ancient salt carriers' route — from the Cheshire salt-mines to Baildon market — which crossed Harden Beck. The huge office block of the Bradford and Bingley Building Society now dominates the town centre. A circular walk from Bingley is described on page 108.

Continue along the towpath from the station; walk under Park Road Bridge towards Three Rise Locks. Notice the enclosed alleyway by allotments which leads under the railway to the area of Bingley around the Parish Church. This is known locally as "Treacle (Trickle) Cock Alley", because of the dripping tap which can still be seen in the tunnel.

You soon reach Three Rise Locks, the first of the two systems of staircase locks for which

Bingley is famous. Almost immediately beyond, past a lovely wooded area of canal, the remarkable Five Rise Locks form a prominent industrial monument. More than two centuries after they were built, these two staircase systems are still considered engineering marvels. A model of both lock systems is kept at the Science Museum in London.

The Five Rise Locks lift the level of the canal a full 60 feet in less than 100 yards. Each lock measures 62 feet by 14 ft 4ins, and they have changed little in appearance since they were constructed in the 1770s by local stonemasons. It can take well over an hour to negotiate the locks, and care is needed to manipulate the massive oak gates in the correct sequence.

These are the last locks you will encounter before Gargrave. There now follows an extended "pound" some 16 miles long, making this one of the most perfectly level walks in the north of England.

The canal now winds gently on a more elevated way through the natural gorge that forms this part of Airedale; you will see the wooded hillside and crags of Druid's Altar rising to the left. You soon pass boatyards and crowded moorings, houses and canalside gardens, to Micklethwaite Bridge which crosses the canal at Crossflatts.

The lane to the left leads down to Crossflatts MetroTrain station, the first of all the new local rail halts to be opened on

West Yorkshire's rail network in the early 1980s; it is now a busy commuter station.

Micklethwaite, a typical small Pennine textile village, lies only half a mile to the right along the lane at Crossflatts. It is now a conservation area. It contains Holroyd Mill, a water-powered mill now renovated and known as Micklethwaite Studio Workshops where a variety of potters, artists and local craftspeople welcome visitors. The workshops are open daily and light refreshments are available.

Beyond Crossflatts the canal enters a busy part of Airedale. It comes close to the old A65, now duplicated by the new Aire Valley trunk road.

Carry on ahead for the next two miles, past Swine Lane to Riddlesden. You'll find the Marquis of Granby, another popular pub close to the canal. There are fine walks from here, via Rivock Edge, over Rombalds Moor to the prehistoric Doubler Stones, and on to Addingham and Ilkley. A short way to the left, and across the main road, is East Riddlesden Hall. This fascinating house, now in the care of the National Trust, was originally a late Elizabethan banqueting hall. It was built in 1602, though the main part of the house was erected in 1648 for James Murgatroyd, a wealthy Halifax clothier and merchant. It is a house of dark stone gables and mullioned windows, which is reputed to be haunted.

The hall has many special features, including the original central hall, a magnificent rose window, Civil War carvings, period fireplaces, oak panelling and decorated plaster ceilings. The west wing, added in 1692 to make the building more symmetrical, was sadly demolished some years ago, but its facade remains to shelter the garden.

It has now been furnished by the National Trust in period style, with paintings and kitchen implements.

East Riddlesden Hall, a fascinating merchant's house, is now in the hands of the National Trust.

There are carefully restored and re-planted Jacobean gardens to the rear of the house, and a shop and coffee house in the old bothy, with its intriguing Civil War Royalist inscriptions. The tithe barn dates back to monastic times, and houses a collection of old farming wagons and agricultural implements.

From here into the centre of Keighley is a walk of about a mile along a busy road, or a short bus-ride. Keighley is a busy textile and engineering town on the confluence of the rivers Aire and Worth, the latter coming down from the Brontë moors.

You'll find a pleasant town centre which is part Victorian, part modern. The main shopping street, Cavendish Street, has kept its elegant canopies. There is also a covered, pedestrianised shopping area, presided over by a statue of Rombald — the legendary rock-hurling giant of nearby Rombalds Moor. There is a fine park, aviary and museum at Cliffe Castle, close to the town centre, and a busy station on the MetroTrain Airedale line which is the terminus of the celebrated Worth Valley steam railway.

If possible, find the time to ride on the Worth Valley line, which runs for four and a half miles along a branch line between Keighley, Haworth and Oxenhope. It is without doubt one of the finest preserved lines in Britain.

Every weekend, and daily throughout July, August and other peak holiday times, superbly restored steam trains ply this line. You will be able to call at stations whose restoration has been meticulous — from the milk churns and luggage on the platform to the period posters — and which have won numerous awards.

The Worth Valley Railway has been used as the location for many film and TV productions, including *Yanks* and *The Railway Children*. For this reason the line may already be unconsciously familiar to many visitors. Nevertheless it is a genuine public transport service, catering for local communities as well as bringing thousands of visitors to Haworth without adding to the traffic congestion.

There is a bookshop at Haworth station, and a cafeteria and large steam locomotive museum at Oxenhope. The museum houses many famous engines, including the Lancashire and Yorkshire 0-6-0 freight locomotive built in 1887, which featured in the film of *The Railway Children*.

Worth Valley trains link up with British Rail Airedale Line services from their own platforms on Keighley station. Through booking facilities are available from many West Yorkshire stations.

Beyond Riddlesden and Stocksbridge, the canal swings away from the main road. Airedale broadens out to become a flat-bottomed valley, now dominated by the new Aire Valley trunk road carrying high-speed traffic. But to the right is a quieter landscape of old farms, dense woodland and a steep backcloth of hillside climbing to the edge of Rombalds Moor — the great massif which divides Airedale from Wharfedale. The famous Aire Gap, one of the most important low-level crossings of the Pennines, is now clearly evident ahead.

The canal deviates from the course of the river, turning northwards around the wooded bluff of Lodge Hill, and heading for the mill chimneys and houses of Silsden. This is a small, compact mill town clustered around the canal and its little moorland beck which forms the centrepiece of the old main street, with a variety of shops, cafés and pubs. Although it has expanded in recent years, with housing estates extending

Right: Nowadays the once busy Leeds-Liverpool canal is a haven for fishermen and wildlife.

up to the hillsides, the town centre is all stone-built, full of character and typical West Riding gritstone.

Should you choose to end your day's ramble here, it is about half a mile's walk along the main road and across the trunk road to the new Steeton station. There are also Yorkshire Rider buses which run direct from the town centre to Keighley and Ilkley.

From Silsden the towpath continues along another very attractive stretch of waterway, almost built into the hillside, to give the walker attractive views across the valley. You soon

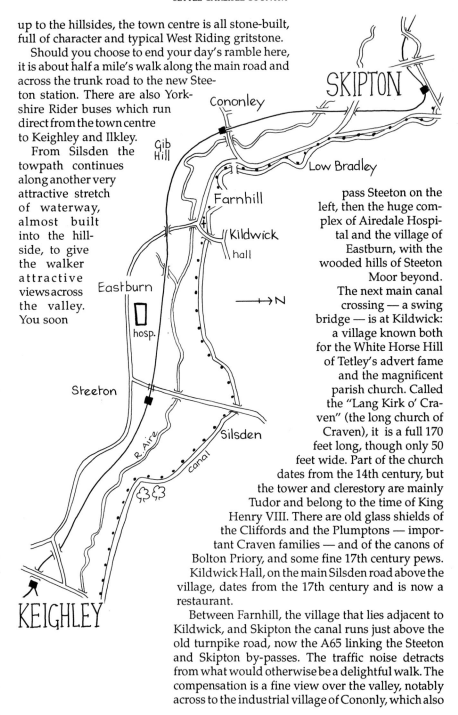

pass Steeton on the left, then the huge complex of Airedale Hospital and the village of Eastburn, with the wooded hills of Steeton Moor beyond. The next main canal crossing — a swing bridge — is at Kildwick: a village known both for the White Horse Hill of Tetley's advert fame and the magnificent parish church. Called the "Lang Kirk o' Craven" (the long church of Craven), it is a full 170 feet long, though only 50 feet wide. Part of the church dates from the 14th century, but the tower and clerestory are mainly Tudor and belong to the time of King Henry VIII. There are old glass shields of the Cliffords and the Plumptons — important Craven families — and of the canons of Bolton Priory, and some fine 17th century pews. Kildwick Hall, on the main Silsden road above the village, dates from the 17th century and is now a restaurant.

Between Farnhill, the village that lies adjacent to Kildwick, and Skipton the canal runs just above the old turnpike road, now the A65 linking the Steeton and Skipton by-passes. The traffic noise detracts from what would otherwise be a delightful walk. The compensation is a fine view over the valley, notably across to the industrial village of Cononly, which also

Skipton's famous castle, the historic seat of the Clifford family, is well worth a visit.

has a reopened Airedale Line station. The lead mining chimney on Gib Hill is a notable landmark. Below Bradley the canal loops around in a great curve to take advantage of the contour, before rejoining the roadside for a straight, fast walk into Skipton.

This isn't the most impressive way into Skipton. Despite fine moorland views to the right, the valley floor is dominated by busy roads, an industrial estate, and then terraced housing. But you soon swing round underneath the massive bridge carrying the branch railway to Embsay and Grassington, which is now a busy freight branch to the lime works at Swinden. You then go under the main road to emerge alongside old wharfs, new housing, a car park and bus station in the centre of Skipton.

Notice the beautifully restored Canal Wharf and warehousing area, complete with old crane, which now forms part of the Dales Outdoor Centre.

Skipton is the perfect place to end a

day's walk. There is an excellent choice of cafés, pubs, shops and accommodation, as well as frequent bus and train services back to West Yorkshire. The railway station, with its beautifully carved stone Midland Railway gryphon crest, is worth a visit in its own right.

The town centre is a superb example of an old Norman town which is still dominated by its ancient and beautifully preserved castle. It is the ancestral home of the Clifford family, and is open daily. The church, filled with tombs of the medieval and Tudor Cliffords, stands close to the great castle gates. The old market street, with its 18th century tollbooth (formerly a gaol) runs down from the castle.

You'll find a busy and colourful street market on every day of the week except Tuesdays (early closing) and Sundays. Many of the medieval "backs" (old town gardens) were developed as courtyards, workshops and terraces during the Industrial Revolution as the Leeds-Liv-

The Leeds-Liverpool Canal runs through the middle of Skipton, but most of the traffic these days is recreational.

erpool Canal — with its cheap coal, imported raw materials and finished goods — encouraged the growth of the textile trade. That trade was in wool and, because of the town's damp climate and canal and rail links with Lancashire, in cotton too.

With the building of steam-powered mills such as Dewhirsts, the old market town was rapidly transformed into a prosperous manufacturing centre. Nevertheless, Skipton has kept its character as a rural market town — with an important sheep and cattle market — and as a focal point of Dales life.

Much of the town's central area has been carefully redeveloped with elegant modern shops, arcades and boutiques. They reflect Skipton's increasingly important role as a busy shopping and administrative centre, as well as a tourist destination. The town is promoted, with some justification, as "The Gateway to the Dales".

Take time, if you can, to visit the excellent Craven Museum on the first floor of the town hall (closed Tuesdays). It contains items which tell much of the town's and Craven's fascinating history, including exhibits about local geology, natural history and the lead mining industry.

But for a real surprise, make your way across the footbridge into the town centre, and along the High Street. At the top end, to the left of the church, you'll find a bridge over the Springs Branch of the canal and a narrow gap in the wall leading down to the Spring Branch towpath. Descend the narrow steps onto the canal bank, usually a crowded area of moorings, but turn left under the road bridge and follow the Springs Branch behind the Castle walls onto a raised section of towpath which runs between Eller Beck and the canal, which here reaches a cul-de-sac.

This partially wooded ravine is rich

in industrial history. On the left is the mill-race which, until recently, powered a waterwheel for Skipton High Corn Mill, traces of which are now part of Ledgard and Wynne's car park.

On the right is the castle, built on a huge defensive cliff. Its overhanging privies once discharged their contents directly into Eller Beck.

Where the canal branch ends are the remains of a wharf fed by a gravity-powered railway; it brought large quantities of limestone from Haw Park Quarries to the canal for the ironworks of Keighley and Leeds. It is a sad reflection of the age in which we live that this material is now conveyed by heavily polluting road transport.

The footpath from the towpath reaches a stony track. If you turn right you will find yourself at the entrance to Skipton Woods, an extensive area of lakes and woodlands which is open every afternoon from 2pm onwards. Turn left along the track to get back into Skipton town centre. ❏

"Flowerpot boats" — Bill and Ben — *spotted at Skipton.*

Skipton to Settle

A 14-mile (25km) walk that accompanies the canal, follows green lanes and visits some delightful Dales villages, before descending into a welcoming market town.

RETURN to the main Leeds-Liverpool Canal towpath by means of the footbridge immediately behind Skipton bus station and the Co-op car park.

The canal winds behind the centre of the town, past the confluence with the Springs branch on the right, and an area of old mill buildings to the left, some in the process of conversion and restoration. To the right are allotments, and Aireville Park stretching away — it is accessible from the second swing bridge.

You are soon overlooking the station with its Midland Railway coat of arms, and the streets of terraced houses terminated by the canal. Ignore the steps leading off left by a stream crossing through a mill-side area rich in atmosphere; you soon pass more sober houses and gardens.

The canal swings to join and run alongside the main road into Skipton from the by-pass. You have to walk about 200 yards along the road — at least there is a footway — until you reach a pedestrian gate. Rejoin the towpath which now swings away from the road and heads underneath the massive concrete struts of the by-pass.

Leaving the traffic noise behind, you now follow a beautiful stretch of canal. The waterway curves around the gentle mound of Hoober Hill to the right, with ever lovelier views through the Aire Gap across to Gargrave. The Leeds-Settle-Carlisle line is prominent in the foreground.

For the first time since leaving Skipton, the River Aire comes into view.

Skipton is unusual among Dales towns, being situated a good half-mile from the main river in the valley. This reflects its history, being neither at a river crossing nor dependent on the river for transport. It occupied instead a strategic and defensive position on the low gap, on ancient routes between Airedale and Wharfedale. The Norman castle took advantage of the steep and defendable natural cliffs above little Eller Beck, the fast-flowing stream which provided water power for the early corn and woollen mills. Steam, coal and cotton brought industry to Skipton, but they came by canal, not by river.

The low hills in the background are largely drumlins: mounds of glacial waste deposited by the glaciers retreating through what is now Airedale. These low green hills are a characteristic feature of this part of Craven. To the right, a beautiful wooded slope rises up to Flasby Fell and its summit of Sharp Haw. This is a popular walk from Skipton or Gargrave; though it climbs only 1,171 feet it offers one of the finest viewpoints in the southern Dales.

The canal now heads northwards towards the busy A65 road past Thorlby Bridge, before bearing northwest and parallel to the road. Highgate Bridge is soon passed, as is the Johnson and Johnson factory with its tall chimney on the outskirts of Gargrave. This famous manufacturer of medical supplies chose a Dales location because of its clean air.

The canal goes under the A65 and reaches the first set of locks since Bingley.

This is an interesting area, close to a former turnpike tollbooth on the main road above. The canal now swings into Gargrave at Ray Bridge.

Look at the interesting warehouses on the right, now used by an agricultural supplier. This is a reminder that Gargrave was once a port. Lead from the Grassington mines was brought here along a new road, built by the Duke of Devonshire in the 1770s. In Gargrave the lead was loaded onto barges and transported to Leeds and Hull, to provide the roofs and drainpipes of London. Coal was also brought in, and calamine (zinc ore) taken out from the Malham Moor mines for smelting into brass as far away as Cheadle in Staffordshire, along the extensive late 18th and early 19th century waterway system.

The canal now goes directly behind Gargrave. At the second bridge, a fenced path, left, leads directly into the village centre where you'll find an excellent choice of cafés and pubs.

Gargrave owes much of its present size and character to two forms of transport: the canal, as already mentioned, and the Keighley-Kendal turnpike road. The road was built in stages during the 18th century, basically to link two important centres of the textile trade: Leeds, the booming upstart of the Industrial Revolution, and Kendal — more established though already in decline.

The old turnpike, upgraded into a modern A-road, is due to be superceded by a linking system of fast bypasses. Gargrave is one of the places that will be by-passed; this will hopefully have a beneficial effect on this lovely part of the walk.

Gargrave has at least two former coaching inns where horses were changed and travellers refreshed. The stage-coaches generated important trades in the village — cooks, bakers, ostlers, farriers and blacksmiths. With its lovely green alongside the River Aire, and its scatter of grey cottages, Gargrave has real charm.

The handsome church is Victorian, apart from its 16th century tower. Remains of an Anglo-Saxon coffin lid and a fragment of a Saxon cross are to be found in the north porch. The late Iain Macleod, Chancellor of the Exchequer in the Heath administration, is buried in the churchyard. He came from the Craven area and died tragically early, while in office.

Gargrave station, some five minutes walk along the Broughton Road, has train services back to Skipton, and on to either Morecambe or Carlisle. It actually predates the Settle-Carlisle line, being part of the "little" North Western Railway. This company was purchased by the mighty Midland Railway in its attempt to forge a route to Scotland. Parts of the original station buildings from the 1840s survive, built in the mock-Elizabethan style characteristic of the line.

The Pennine Way, Britain's first long-distance footpath, passes through Gargrave on its 250-mile journey from Edale in Derbyshire to Kirk Yetholm in Scotland. Our route finally leaves the Leeds-Liverpool Canal at the third bridge in Gargrave, before the next set of locks; it turns right along West Lane, and joins the Pennine Way. Fork left along the narrow lane which bears around the walls of Gargrave House.

This lane becomes a pleasant tarmac track and climbs past woodland. It turns into a stony track and leaves the Pennine Way which bears right through a stile on its journey to Malham. The track — Mark House Lane — climbs steadily past Harrows Laithe ("laithe" is a dialect word, meaning a barn) and up the side of Heber Hill.

This track is, in fact, the old pre-turnpike highway from Leeds to Kendal, climbing between the drumlins to give fine views of the summit of the Aire gap. Where the track swings sharp left downhill, a gap stile on the right gives access along a path to Haw Crag, from where there is a superb view up to the head of Malhamdale. In fine weather the pale limestone crags glisten magically.

Mark House Lane descends to cross the now narrow River Aire at Bell Busk. Just as the canal has been left for the first time since leaving Leeds, so the route now leaves the River Aire behind, crossing the low watershed to the Upper Ribble valley.

Keep ahead at the crossroads, past Raven Flatt Farm to the hamlet of Bell Busk. The origin of its name is uncertain, but it may well have been the name given to an early inn, as a bush or a "busk" was, from medieval times, used as an inn-sign — hence the sign of the Bell. No inn has been recorded for centuries, though there was, until the 1950s, a railway station here — "Bell Busk for Malham".

Though it was a good four miles from this Dales village, the station was well used during the summer months by visitors who thought nothing of making the eight-mile round-trip on foot, or

Gargrave is a popular watering hole for the the latterday bargees who now ply the Leeds-Liverpool Canal purely for pleasure.

perhaps by the pony and trap service which carried wealthier folk to and from Malham. There is still a direct bridleway to the village of Airton; it is a delightful walk, though far less busy than in the days when excursion trains pulled up at the little station. The station buildings, also in mock-Tudor style, survive as a private house, probably best seen (so as not to intrude on the owners' privacy) from the train.

Beyond Bell Busk, the old Kendal road continues as a pleasant level lane curving alongside one of the becks which forms a tributary of the Aire. The lane bends away from the railway; when it veers to the left again, 500 yards beyond Bell Busk, an optional loop can be made by taking the public path which fords the stream (only crossable in comfort after dry weather). The path goes through a gate by a copse before climbing Kendal Hill to Kendal House farm, which is empty at time of writing. From

here there are impressive views across typical Lower Dales countryside. The rolling drumlins, of which Kendal Hill is one, are much in evidence, as is the sharp peak of Sharp Haw to the southeast.

The path returns to the road; it goes through a field gate and alongside the hedge to the corner of the field. Turn right into Otterburn, a hamlet whose name and beck — which still flows into the Aire — evokes an animal once common in the Dales. The otter is now virtually extinct in this part of England, thanks to ruthless hunting and the impact of pesticides.

Otterburn is a small farming community which enjoys a beautiful, unspoiled setting. Turn left at the crossroads; almost immediately a gate on the right leads into a track, Dacre Lane. Keep right around the edge of a little copse, and climb to a higher plantation ahead. Go through it and past the woodland on

Wenningber Hill into a large, open field.

If you decide to end this stage at Hellifield, you swing to the southwest here across the field, to a field gate in the wall ahead near a barn. This leads to a track which eventually becomes a walled lane, Haw Lane, leading underneath the railway to Hellifield.

Hellifield was once the Crewe of the Settle-Carlisle line: a bustling railway junction where the prosperous Lancashire and Yorkshire Railway from Manchester (Victoria), Blackburn and Clitheroe met the mighty Midland to feed into the latter's route to Scotland.

The decline of the Ribble Valley services must be one of the gloomiest stories of bureaucratic mismanagement in northern transport history. Happily this decline is about to be reversed, thanks to the initiatives of both Lancashire County Council and British Rail. An experimental Sunday service was due to start in summer 1990, to be followed, hopefully, by the restoration of a regular service between Hellifield, Clitheroe, Whalley and Blackburn to meet the huge new demand for a form of transport that is an alternative to the increasingly congested roads. Of these stations, Clitheroe, like many stations on the Settle-Carlisle line, was reopened to DalesRail trains in the 1970s. Whalley, too, is due to be reopened.

But Hellifield will never again enjoy the great glories of the steam years, when crowded trains filled the huge canopied station. There were magnificent refreshment rooms (First and Third Class) with well-stocked cellars of beer and fine wines. The station master and an army of enginemen, porters, signalmen and traffic clerks looked after the needs of the passengers travelling through this busy junction station.

The engine shed has long since disappeared; it was here that locomotives of two companies were stabled, before taking almost non-stop freight and passenger trains to destinations in Lancashire, Yorkshire or Scotland. Juggernauts now crowd the motorways and trunk roads to produce quite appalling levels of congestion and pollution.

The station, with its magnificent glass canopies and ironwork emblazoned with Midland Railway gryphons, is a Listed Building. Nevertheless it is in a sadly neglected state, and its future looks bleak unless a positive new use can be found for it — ideally connected with its rich railway heritage.

In addition to its long terraces of railwaymens' cottages, Hellifield still has an old village centre, with a post office and comfortable inn. You'll also find an example of a pele tower about half a mile south of the village, just off the Clitheroe road. It is unusual to find one so far south, since they were built to withstand the onslaughts of Scottish raiders. While there is no public access to the tower, a public path goes alongside it.

Return to the main Settle-Carlisle Way, at Dacre Lane. You should keep in the same direction as you walked from Otterburn, to the right of a small plantation to a gate and into a field with a wall on your left. Go through the next field gate, onto Hellifield Moor Top. Keeping a wall to your right, pass a barn and cross into an open field; the track is now faint on the ground. Keep on to a field gate, over a natural pass between low hills — the track eventually becomes a walled lane.

This is Langber Lane, one of the finest of the old Dales roads, providing superb, easy walking. Keep ahead for a good mile past Bookilber Barn. If you want to make a detour to Long Preston, take a field path to the left here. Long Preston has a railway station, two excellent pubs, a large village green with a maypole and a Rohan shop which sells outdoor gear.

Otherwise, Langber Lane takes you

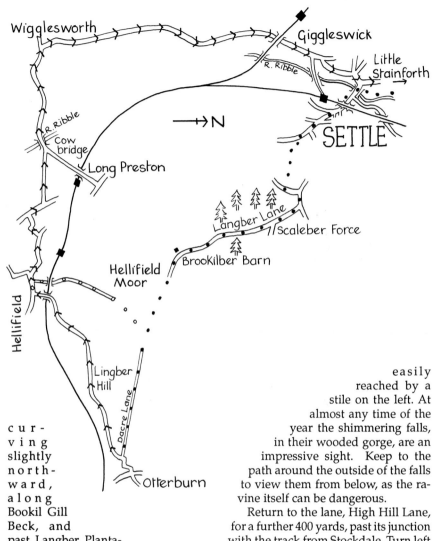

curving slightly northward, along Bookil Gill Beck, and past Langber Plantation on the right, the track picking out the natural line of the valley. Ahead and to the left is a large plantation, known as Wild Share. Carry on until you reach the minor road from Airton and Kirkby Malham.

Continue in the same direction along the road for a further 400 yards to reach Scaleber Force, an exquisite waterfall easily reached by a stile on the left. At almost any time of the year the shimmering falls, in their wooded gorge, are an impressive sight. Keep to the path around the outside of the falls to view them from below, as the ravine itself can be dangerous.

Return to the lane, High Hill Lane, for a further 400 yards, past its junction with the track from Stockdale. Turn left after a further 100 yards along a track, Lambert Lane. Go 200 yards along the track and take a stile on your right. This leads to a path that runs along the edge of a series of fields, contouring around the hillside above Settle. It finally curves left, then sharp right, to a plantation above a little reservoir. Turn left again here, to swing round the outside of the

The delightfuly ornate folly, in the conservation area just off Settle market place

reservoir and join Mitchell Lane as it descends into upper Settle. You join a lane above crowded cottage rooftops, then drop suddenly and steeply into Settle town.

After a long day's walk, there can be few more welcoming places in the Dales than Settle. It is full of character and lies in a superb setting of limestone scenery. You'll find Jacobean and Georgian cottages and houses, courtyards and narrow alleyways, plus the Folly, an architectural extravaganza of a town house dating from 1675. You will see it on your right just before you reach the marketplace.

Market day — always a colourful event — is Tuesday. The market square contains both a cross and the unusual three-decker Shambles (an old name for butchers' shops), with shops on two

levels below their accommodation. The Tourist Information Centre is next to the handsome Victorian French-style town hall.

Don't miss the Museum of North Craven Life in Chapel Place, close to the town centre, which has superbly presented displays of local history, archaeology and culture. You can see some of the finds from Victoria Cave (a walk to the cave is described on page 118) and mementos of famous visitors to Settle, including the composer Edward Elgar. Linton Court, just off Duke Street, is worth visiting for its frequent photographic and art exhibitions.

Right: The 236 miles to London must have seemed a frightening prospect when this stone was erected at Settle back in the stage coach days.

Two particularly important people came from Settle. George Birkbeck, 1776-1841, the son of a local banker and merchant, founded the Mechanics' Institutes in Glasgow and London (Birkbeck College in London is named after him). Edwin Waugh (1839-1908) was a social reformer and philanthropist, founder of the National Society for the Prevention of Cruelty to Children.

If you still have sufficient energy after your day's ramble, make your way to Castle Street, behind the TSB. A doorway in the street wall leads to a footpath that winds its way steeply to the summit of Castlebergh — the limestone crag that towers over Settle. It offers a truly magnificent panorama over the rooftops of the town and across Upper Ribblesdale to the Forest of Bowland — the green copper dome of Giggleswick School chapel being a notable landmark in the foreground.

Settle is well supplied with excellent pubs, cafés and shops to meet the needs of tired walkers. There's a good bookshop and even a choice of outdoor shops in case anything has worn out on the tramp from Skipton.

Settle station is, of course, one of the most famous on the Settle-Carlisle line. It is a perfect example of a small Midland Railway station and one that is, for once, in an almost perfect state of preservation. The architectural style is "Derby Gothic", with beautifully kept gardens. You will find that all too rare commodity on rural (and even urban) stations in the 1990s — station staff — at least during the earlier part of the day. They are invariably helpful.

● **CYCLE TRAIL:** The route takes you through the hamlets of Stirton and Thorlby, before joining the A65 trunk road. Just before the riverside village of Gargrave, there is a minor road, right, signed "Flasby". Go right, soon, as you join another road, then bear next left to enjoy easy riding to the pleasant village of Airton, set around a spacious green.

The minor road continues through Otterburn and thence to Hellifield; don't neglect to inspect the canopied railway station. You rejoin the busy A65 road — but only briefly — before taking off left along minor roads to Wigglesworth. From here to Settle, you are riding parallel to a long distance footpath known as the Ribble Way. ❏

Settle to Ribblehead

A 15-mile (24km) walk through some of the finest limestone scenery in the Craven Dales, finishing at a stunning example of railway engineering.

THIS day's walk takes in some of the most spectacular scenery in the Craven Dales, and many fascinating historic features. The route to Horton-in-Ribblesdale largely follows the Ribblesdale Way, and the town can provide a convenient break if the full day's walk might prove too strenuous. This will leave a more manageable nine miles to Ribblehead for those less energetically inclined.

From Settle market-place follow Kirkgate due west, towards the top end of the car park by the railway. Before reaching Victoria Hall, turn sharp right, after Dugdale's shop, down a narrow, high-walled ginnel marked by a "no cycling" sign, which takes you alongside the high brick viaduct carrying the Settle-Carlisle line.

When this path reaches the main road, turn left and walk across the river bridge. Almost immediately over the bridge take a path to the right which follows a fenced way around a playing field. Continue along the path to a stile, and then across a small field to the next stile and along an embankment. This is a particularily attractive section of path, with the river below.

Across the river is the complex of Langcliffe Mill, now mainly a caravan park, but containing some interesting 18th century mill buildings. It is one of several water-powered mills in this part of Ribblesdale. The path then crosses another field to join the lane below Stackhouse at a stile. But almost immediately

opposite, another stile leads to a path alongside the wall, parallel with the lane, towards Stackhouse.

Stackhouse is a hamlet almost totally enclosed within dry-stone walls. As the path reaches the corner of the enclosure, go through the gate back onto the lane, but take the first track left through the hamlet past gardens and cottages. Turn right at the first junction, then right again at the second to rejoin the lane. Bear very slightly left, to a track which descends to the river, cottages and weir at Langcliffe. Notice the fine salmon leap where, at the right season of the year, these magnificent fish can be seen in action. The weir once provided water power for Langcliffe Mill.

The route continues along the footpath on the far side of the river, across a steep step stile, then a series of riverside stiles, to arrive on the B6479 just below Robert's Paper Mill.

Walk along the road for about 100 yards before turning right along the lane which is the entrance to Langcliffe Tip. Immediately after going under the railway, look for a stepped path on the left which runs alongside the railway embankment. This goes into the tip yard to reach the famous Hoffman Kiln at Langcliffe.

This remarkable industrial monument is one of only two in Britain to survive more or less intact. It was an unusual, yet efficient, form of limekiln, burning the lime by means of a continu-

The ancient packhorse bridge at Stainforth, one of the narrowest in the Dales, is crossed by our cycle route and well worth a detour for walkers.

ous fire which operated over a gigantic oval tunnel-oven. Coal and limestone were burned on a continual loading process, the hydrated lime being loaded into waiting rail wagons.

Though the kiln has long been obsolete, Craven District Council has resolved to stabilise the structure. There are plans to interpret the area and open it up for visitors as part of the ambitious Ribblesdale Project. At the time of writing, however, there is no public access to the kiln without permission of the council, for safety reasons. But the public path runs close by, so you can easily look inside the kiln through one of the side ports. You will see the magnificent structure which has been compared, in the scale and elegance of its brick arches, with the great Cellarium at Fountains Abbey.

The path goes to the left of the kiln over a little footbridge, and continues as

a pleasant field path parallel to the railway, marked by stiles. You emerge on the main road just north of Stainforth Youth Hostel at Taitlands. Bear left, after 150 yards, along the road into Stainforth village.

Since it was by-passed some years ago, Stainforth is now spared the noise and disruption of quarry wagons. It is once again a quiet little backwater of pleasing cottages, a shop and a pub, an early Victorian church and a delightful beck with stepping stones.

The original "Stainforth" or "stony ford" undoubtedly refers to a crossing over the river some 200 yards west of the village, between "Little" or "Knight" Stainforth with its handsome 17th century hall, and Great Stainforth, as the present village was sometimes known. It is worth crossing the main road by the underpass built for local school children and continuing a further 100 yards

up the road to take the lane, left, to reach the magnificent Stainforth packhorse bridge.

This structure, narrow enough to slow drivers down to walking pace, replaced the ford, probably in monastic times, when Stainforth lay on an major packhorse route between the important ports of Lancaster, York and Ripon. The present bridge, which dates from the 17th century, is now owned by the National Trust and is just a few yards from a waterfall: Stainforth Force.

For the energetic, another very special place to visit from Stainforth is Catrigg Force, accessible along the stony track, Goat Lane, reached either across the stepping stones or from the "back" of the village. This is an extremely steep ascent, but worth every ounce of effort. At the top of the track a stile gives access to a footpath which leads both to the top and the base of the waterfall. It is a narrow, shimmering column of water which, in the opinion of many cognoscenti, is the prettiest waterfall in the entire Yorkshire Dales, particularily after frost when icicles and frozen spray can create complex patterns.

Back to the main route, take the left of two paths that start just east of Stainforth Church, waymarked "Pen y Ghent". This path crosses a field, then bears right and climbs steeply up across pasture above Haw Beck. Keep straight ahead, alongside a field wall to the left, across two open fields. Then follow a wall first to the left and then to the right to join a track, Moor Head Lane.

Turn left along this enclosed green lane, down to its eventual junction with the main road at Helwith Bridge. Follow the road with care for 100 yards, before turn-

53

Sorry — no road for sheep! Note the Ribble Way marker on this national park signpost, near Stainforth.

ing right at the junction. Cross over the railway line to Helwith Bridge itself, and a welcoming pub.

The route continues on the far side of the pub, following a walled track along the edge of fields to swing back under the railway to the riverside. Walk northwards to avoid a large bend in the river, as the track becomes a field path leading to Crag Hill Farm by the river. The path continues along the riverside, another attractive stretch. You walk away from the river where it bends, past lovely riverside meadows, to reach Horton at the end of the bridge.

Horton-in-Ribblesdale — to give it the full title — is a convenient rest and refreshment point on the walk. If your feet ache you can also catch a train from here. The Crown Inn, just across the bridge, offers accommodation, food and Theakston's Bitter, while another pub, the Golden Lion, reopened recently. The excellent Pen y Ghent Stores and Café,

further along the main road in the village, is a mecca for walkers. You can cradle a mug of tea, enjoy first class food at prices ramblers can afford, and browse through displays of maps, books and outdoor equipment. There is also a village shop and post office.

Though nearby quarries and their wagons have spoiled the village centre, there are still some fascinating corners to explore.

Horton's medieval parish church is particularily interesting. It is Perpendicular in style, dating from the 15th century, but with many Norman features, including the south doorway and font.

There is also a beautifully kept railway station, worth seeing for its garden alone; it is maintained, like many others on the line, by local volunteers and the Friends of the Settle-Carlisle line. The timetable will remind you of services back to Settle, Skipton or Leeds (or even

Blackburn and Manchester) or forward to Carlisle.

Go west along the path at the rear of the station which crosses to a stile, and then bears right alongside a wall. This is part of the 24-mile Three Peaks Walk and is easy to follow. Keep straight ahead to a ladder stile below Beecroft Hall Farm, crossing the next field to a further stile. The way now climbs steadily, bearing left through the next gap and up into a deep groove through the limestone pasture. This is Sulber Nick — thought to be of Iron Age origin, and perhaps the main route to the ancient hill fort, the remains of which can still be traced on the summit of Ingleborough. There are a number of ancient field systems which can be traced in the moorland hereabouts.

Beyond the nick you reach a well-signed crossing of tracks on a high moorland plateau. There are spectacular views all around, particularly of Pen y Ghent. Turn right here, and head down towards a field gate. Pass above South House Farm before going through the next gate. The route now bears left, away from the bridleway, along the outside of the wall to the next gateway, above Borrins and Gill Garth farms, to go through a gate and onto an enclosed track.

At the corner of this track a stile leads to a footpath to the huge, impressive canyon of Alum Pot. This is a private path, and a small admission fee is payable at Selside Farm before you investigate the pothole. The farm is a short distance further down the track, and immediately to the right.

Alum Pot is one of the most spectacular potholes in the Pennines: a huge, gaping hole surrounded by trees, with fuming waterfalls. It is 100 yards deep, and links with an exten-

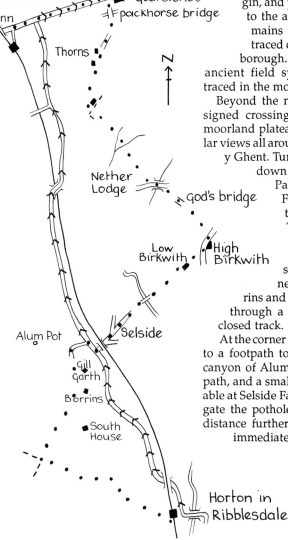

sive cave and pothole system. Early writers imagined it to be an entrance to Hell itself, the waterfall spray being the smoke of Hellfire. The first descent of "Hell" by rope was made in 1847.

Return the same way down the track to reach the main B6479 road at Selside. Turn right through the hamlet, then left along a track which soon crosses under the railway. Avoid tracks which fork right and left, keeping straight on along the aptly named Drain Mires Lane. Negotiate the ladder stile at the bottom of the lane, keeping left over the footbridge across the Ribble.

From here follow the footpath by the stream over a couple of stiles to Low Birkwith Farm. Keep ahead past the farmhouse, crossing the stile to the rear and following the path up to the next stile and little wood below High Birkwith. Go over another stile to rejoin the Pennine Way (last encountered at Gargrave) just below Birkwith Farm.

About 150 yards along the track, bear left along a path; it follows the wall to the left, below the slope of the hill. This emerges at God's Bridge — a huge slab of limestone which forms a convenient, and natural, crossing of the beck. There are several such examples in the Pennines.

Cross the pasture, bearing left to a gateway leading across the bridge over Cam Beck by Nether Lodge Farm. Once through the farmyard, the path leaves the farm track to cross straight ahead over open pasture, climbing the low hill ahead, at the far side of which a stile crosses the wall. Keep ahead in the same direction, across a rather boggy area of rough pasture, crossing the becks which form Crutchin Gill ahead.

Ascend the other side of the shallow dip. Head for the gate ahead, above the gill, now following the wall around, still on rough pasture. Make for the barn, left, going through the gate, around the barn to the right then keep the wall on

the right as you head for the next gateway, descending to the deserted hamlet of Thorns. This settlement is now reduced to a couple of ruined farmhouses and barns. As recently as the 1930s it was a thriving community, with regular village dances.

Go left on the enclosed track, Thorns Lane, but bear right at the fork, soon climbing an open field to another gateway, from where the path descends to Thorns Gill. Gayle Beck, which flows through the narrow and exquisitely beautiful ravine of Thorns Gill, is one of the principal sources of the River Ribble. The beautiful little packhorse bridge over the gill dates from the early 17th century, and formed part of the ancient Craven Way packhorse route between the townships of Settle and Dent in days before turnpike roads and railways.

Cross the bridge carefully, and follow the wall uphill above the gill, through pedestrian gates to the main road at Gearstones. The cottages to the right, where there is now simple accommodation for walkers, was once part of a famous drovers' inn, used by Scottish drovers in the 18th century on their way to the cities of the North and Midlands, with vast herds of Galloway or Ayrshire cattle for hungry markets.

From here it is only a short walk along the road to Ribblehead, a bleak yet beautiful landscape dominated by the magnificent 24-arch viaduct whose future still remains a critical factor in the survival of the Leeds-Settle-Carlisle railway. Welcome repairs in recent months now suggest that the viaduct and the railway will survive for some years to come, both as a great monument to the Railway Age and as part of a working railway.

Only the southbound platform survives at Ribblehead Station, the other having been demolished to make way for a quarry siding. However there are plans either to make a second platform

The splendid isolation of Ribblehead Viaduct has inspired a variety of activities, including free rock concerts which earned the attentions of the law. Less controversial is the revival of the traditional sheep show.

or to single the track south of the station to permit northbound trains to call. This would be a boon to walkers.

In the meantime, rest and refreshment are available at the Station Inn. Allow a good five minutes to walk from the pub up the long station drive to the platform at the end of the viaduct. Ribblehead has perhaps the loneliest commuter train service in England, with an 0659 train for Leeds on which there is unlikely ever to be a rush for seats!

● **CYCLE TRAIL:** The route is along the A65 road to Kendal, but only just over the Ribble Bridge in Settle. Take the first road on your right, which takes you through the village of Stackhouse to Little Stainforth. Turn right here, past the hall, to cross the river by the old packhorse bridge to Stainforth. Spend a little time exploring the village — beyond the main road — before following the B6479 to Helwith Bridge (pub just off the route to the left) and Horton-in Ribblesdale, where the Pen y Ghent café makes a good stop for refreshments.

North of Horton, the landscape becomes wilder, as you approach the junction of roads by the famous Ribblehead viaduct. ❑

Ribblehead to Garsdale

A nine-mile (16km) walk across the fells, in the shadow of Whernside, with extensive views in to the lovely valley of Dentdale , the reward after a lonely moorland stretch.

STARTING a walk from Ribblehead can be a problem if you live to the south of the Yorkshire Dales, at a time when northbound trains from Skipton and Leeds can no longer call at the station.

Aware of the problem, British Rail normally allows Ribblehead-bound passengers to change trains at Dent or Garsdale and catch the next southbound service, hopefully without too long a wait in an unheated waiting room. Check the times of services carefully if you are coming out by train. Let's hope the intended restoration of the northbound platform is not too far off.

From Ribblehead station, cross to the Station Inn and take any of the tracks over the common alongside the monumental and much-photographed viaduct to the central arches, which are as impressive in close-up as they are from a distance. If the wind is blowing strongly through the arches, it is easy to imagine the occasion when a car was blown off a passing train. It is less easy to believe that a driver's cap was blown off his head, underneath the arches to land back on his head from the other side—a tale that probably owes more to the excellent ales of the Station Inn than to any meteorological marvels!

One thing is beyond dispute: that Ribblehead is one of the coldest and wettest points served by railway in England. It thus makes a better place to start a walk than to finish one. That said, there can be superb days, even in winter, of clear skies, when nearby Cam Fell and Ingleborough itself can gleam with a remarkable sharpness and clarity. This great, treeless landscape is one of epic beauty, and even wild and stormy days can have a poetry of their own, if you are well clad and a train is due fairly soon.

The path continues alongside the viaduct, climbing the other side of the dip. It follows the track-bed of one of the many old tramways that snaked through the shanty towns of Batty Moss, which is where many of the navvies lived when the viaduct and nearby Blea Moor tunnel were being built during the 1870s. It must have been a wild, rip-roaring place, with even a tale of a wife being sold for the price of a barrel of beer going undisputed. There were missionaries to cater for the mens' spiritual needs, though they probably had an easier time of it in darkest Africa.

There are still traces in the grassy moorland of both work-sites and the old shanty towns, which gloried in names such as Sebastapol and Inkerman, Jerusalem and Jericho — with echoes of both the Old Testament and the Crimean War.

The path soon becomes a good track, part of it restored with an excellent surface as part of the Three Peaks project. The route goes past the signal box, reputed to be one of the loneliest in England. It is still very much in service, controlling this key central section of the railway and an important passing loop, as well as the single section of track over the viaduct itself.

The track ascends a low hillock, Blue Clay Ridge, then dips down. Keep straight ahead over a difficult area of crossing streams, picking the line of a path veering off slightly right as the main Three Peaks and Whernside road swings left over the aqueduct that crosses the railway at Little Dale.

The route lies directly ahead over a stile along the line of Blea Moor Tunnel. Waymarks could not be more obvious: huge round ventilation shafts with their attendant spoil tips that dominate the landscape in front of you.

Blea Moor Tunnel, 2629 yards long and up to 500 feet below the surface of the moor, is another of the great engineering features of the Leeds-Settle-Carlisle railway. The tunnel was accessed by these great shafts, up which spoil was carried by steam powered cranes. Remains of the winding houses can still be seen.

The path is easy to follow to the summit of Blea Moor, with Blea Moor Crags to

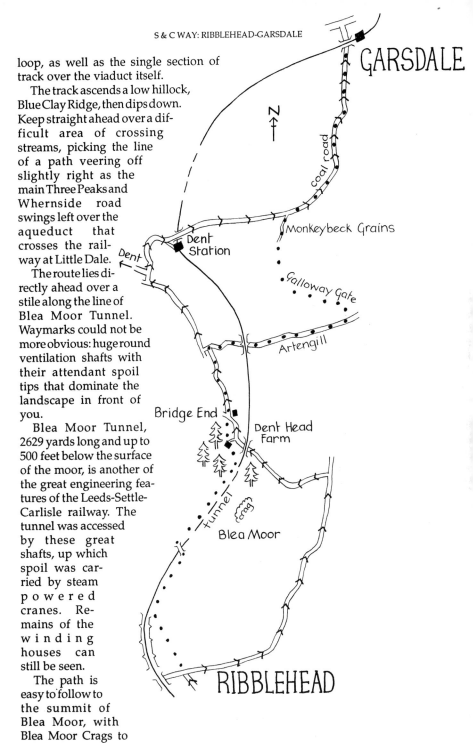

GARSDALE

N

Coal road

Monkeybeck Grains

Dent Station

Dent

Galloway Gate

Artengill

Bridge End

Dent Head Farm

Tunnel

Crag

Blea Moor

RIBBLEHEAD

the right, and extensive views down into Dentdale and to the summit of Whernside, a great whale-back of a ridge, which curves away to the left.

Descend to yet another air shaft and carry straight on to a forest plantation. There are superb views from here of the railway as it curves through Dentdale, past Dent Head and Artengill viaducts, contouring around the high fellside in impressive style.

The path goes over a stile and descends into the wood along a fire break. Keep ahead to the stile at the bottom of the wood, which lies immediately over the northern mouth of Blea Moor tunnel.

You emerge in an area of spoil-heaps, partially covered with heather. The path curves to the left over mounds and along a narrow artificial ridge made of spoil, before crossing a bridge made from sleepers and plunging down to a beck. Keep ahead and cross a footbridge. The path goes past the front of Dent Head Farm, a traditional Dales farmhouse in a secluded and isolated setting. No-one lives here now, though it is still part of a working farm.

Cross back over the stream below the farm, contouring along the hillside to the right before steadily descending to a stile. It gives access to another bridge, this time over the River Dee at Bridge End.

Turn left into the lane. You have now joined another long distance footpath, the Dales Way, on its 81-mile journey from Ilkley to Windermere, beside the rivers Wharfe, Dee, Lune, and Kent. Though this is road walking, the lane is generally quiet, and charming, with the little River Dee running past old farms. You will soon pass Dent Head Youth Hostel on the left.

Stone House Farm is next; it lies immediately below Artengill viaduct, another of the impressive feats of engineering along the Settle-Carlisle line. If

in need of refreshment, you can continue along the road for just 500 yards until you see the welcoming sign of the Sportsman's Inn. Otherwise, turn right at Stone House Farm to join a track past another farm.

You will see the remains of old workings which once produced "Dent marble", a highly fossilised black limestone which derives its colour from a high carbon content. It was popular in late Victorian times for cutting and polishing into highly attractive table-tops and mantelpieces. Examples were to be found in stations along the Settle-Carlisle line until they were snapped up by collectors. However, the outdoor centre of Ingleborough Hall, in Clapham, has two magnificent indoor columns made of this distinctive rock.

Now begins an ascent of Artengill, the massive viaduct you see ahead. It is 600 feet high, with eleven columns. If you are lucky enough to see a train going across as you climb, it will make an unforgettable sight. You will get a vivid impression of the heroic scale of the railway engineering, and the grandeur of the landscape through which the line passes.

You will have plenty of time to inspect the great pillars and arches as you climb a stony path, part of an ancient highway which crosses from Dentdale into Widdale and Wensleydale. Despite the gradient this is a rewarding climb, up to and finally above the railway line up the steep hillside.

Almost at the summit of the pass you join Galloway Gate, a broad track coming in at an acute angle on the left, along the shoulder of Great Knoutberry Hill.

Take this track, climbing sharply upwards before levelling out to contour at high level, around the edge of the fell. You go through gates and past ancient coal pits, on a route running parallel with the valley. You will get magnificent panoramic views across to Whernside

North of Ribblehead, the route follows the railway closely as far as the lonely signal box on Blea Moor, where the extensive trackwork is a reminder of the days when extra locomotives would be used on the Long Drag from Settle, to be put in sidings here. The picture shows a morning Leeds-Carlisle train, with the distinctive shape of Ingleborough in the background.

and Gregareth, down Dentdale, with the smooth contours of the Howgill Hills as a backdrop. In good weather you will see well beyond even these beautiful hills to the the Langdale Pikes and other Lakeland peaks. This is arguably the best viewpoint on the entire Settle-Carlisle Way.

The name "Galloway Gate" indicates the track's origin, for it is one of the network of great drove roads which came down from Galloway in Southern Scotland, avoiding the turnpike roads. The breadth of this old road indicates its value for droving, with ample grazing at the edges. This characterful track gradually descends to meet the tarmac road from Dent Station above Monkeybeck Grains.

If you want to end this section of the walk at Dent station, you should turn left along this road. The station — at 1,100 feet above sea level, the highest mainline station in England — is a superb viewpoint in its own right. The little station-master's house, above the station, is believed to be the first house in England to have double-glazing, such is the ferocity of the westerly gales here.

Though part of the station itself is private, and is being renovated, the "up" waiting room has been restored by the Friends of the Settle-Carlisle line. It offers very necessary shelter for waiting travellers in an otherwise very exposed position. But there can be few more romantic place to wait for a train on a winter's evening when, with lights ablaze, a Class 47 or 31 locomotive suddenly appears around the corner with its rake of warm, brightly-lit coaches.

Diesel railcars, when they return in the form of Sprinters, will inevitably stir less emotion. But at least the station has the benefit of tall station lights, which are angled to light up both platforms.

To continue on to Garsdale you turn right along the road (instead of going left down to Dent station). This is the Coal Road, another ancient track and part of Galloway Gate, which gave access to the coal pits on the summit of the pass. At one time, coal was carried down by pack-pony to supply both Dentdale and Garsdale.

The road rises to more than 1,700 feet above sea level, making this the highest point on the whole route between Leeds and Carlisle. Again there are magnificent views of the surrounding fell country as the road levels out, curves round and finally drops steeply into Garsdale, with Garsdale station and its attendant cottages almost immediately below.

Garsdale station is perhaps the busi-est of the specially reopened halts on the Settle-Carlisle line. It was, until 1959, an important junction station, with trains for Hawes, Aysgarth and Northallerton meeting Leeds-Carlisle trains, and even a through train from Bradford to Hawes. Indeed, it was once known as Hawes Junction.

Both of the waiting rooms have been restored. The one on the down line is now a small information centre, with a good supply of leaflets and brochures about local tourist attractions. There is even the luxury of toilets with more or less running water.

Even though the grand canopies have gone, there is still a sense of importance about the station. Steam engines stop here to fill up with the pure water from a nearby moorland stream (and to be

The lush green contours of Dentdale seem a different world after crossing the watershed from Blea Moor.

The road from Ribblehead towards Hawes, followed by our cycle route, crosses bleak moorland, strewn with the debris of the last Ice Age. There are occasional havens, like this walkers' shelter, near Gearstones.

photographed after the long "drag" from either Settle or Appleby). Once there were water pick-up troughs where expresses could gather water at speed, fed from a great water tank which had sufficient space underneath to serve as a village hall.

There are still some grass-covered sidings, sadly never used, and the site of the old turntable (now at the Worth Valley Railway) where a steam locomotive was once caught by a gust of wind and spun for hours until it was halted by pouring sand into the works. After this incident a palisade was constructed around the turntable, to avoid a repetition.

There are few facilities for tired walkers at Garsdale Station, though you can walk to the Moorcock Inn — on the A684 to Hawes, at the junction with the Kirkby Stephen road — in just twenty minutes.

It is also an easy trip to the delightful little market town of Hawes, where pubs,

The Duchess of Hamilton crosses Dandry Mire viaduct as it approaches Garsdale Station from Carlisle.

restaurants and overnight accommodation are plentiful. Transport is no longer by train — the Wensleydale line having been closed — but by minibuses which meet certain morning and afternoon trains in both directions. With careful planning you can end the walk at Garsdale Station to catch a late afternoon minibus to Hawes, and return in a minibus to Garsdale the next morning to restart the walk.

A walk from Garsdale station to Hawes is described on page 132.

● **CYCLE TRAIL:** Leave Ribblehead by the road to Hawes; for the next few miles you ride through a landscape inhabited mainly by hardy Dales sheep.

Take the road, left, signposted to Dent. The road soon goes steeply downhill , passing beneath the railway immediately to the south of Dent Head viaduct,

to follow the river Dee, passing Artengill Viaduct, high up on the right as you swing left across the river. You pass the Sportsman's pub on the left, and, half a mile further on, take the Garsdale road to the right, which climbs steeply past Dent station. After some high-level moorland pedalling, the old Coal Road descends almost as steeply to Garsdale station. ❏

The City of Wells is pictured, **above**, leaving Rise Hill tunnel. Between here and Blea Moor the line is built on a shallow shelf on the fellside high above Dentdale, a shown in the view, **below**, of the Duchess of Hamilton approaching Dent Station from the south.

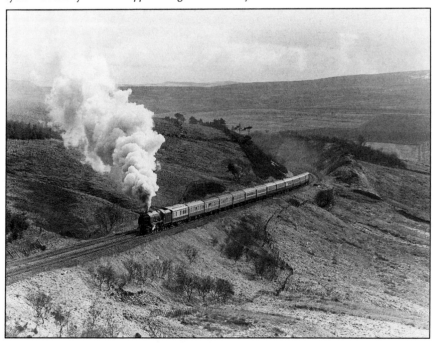

Garsdale to Kirkby Stephen

A 13-mile (23km) walk from the source of the Eden down the spectacular Mallerstang valley, by way of the ancient track used by the redoubtable Lady Anne Clifford.

THIS section of the walk is sometimes known as Lady Anne Clifford's Way, following as it does part of the ancient High Way, a green track dating from the Bronze Age, used by the remarkable Lady Anne on her journeys from Skipton to her castles at Pendragon, Brough and Appleby.

It crosses the watershed between Ure and Eden, the summit of the Settle-Carlisle line, and follows the length of the Mallerstang valley, one of the most dramatic stretches of landscape through which the railway travels. You walk between the massive escarpments of Wild Boar Fell and Mallerstang Edge — both superb fell walks for the experienced hiker.

From Garsdale Station go down the station drive, turning right along the Hawes road for about 200 yards. Look for a gap stile on the left, just past a field gate. Cross rough pasture uphill to a gap in the wall above, then bear half right to a stile in the wall corner. Keep straight ahead across a shallow dip to the next stile, then head down the hillside. As soon as the footbridge over the railway line comes into view, make directly for it, crossing the remains of a wall. Go over the footbridge but immediately turn left off the track to the cottages at the main road opposite. To the right of these buildings is a narrow stile.

Left: The fells above Dent.

Go through it, heading for the stile to the left of the wall corner below, by a barn.

Now bear left to the corner of the next field where the stile gives access to a little footbridge over the infant River Ure. Cross to a gate, then negotiate a stile ahead. Go left here along the wallside, crossing a beck to a stile a few yards from the wall corner. The path now climbs up a low hill to another stile on the brow of the hill. From here you can see tiny Lunds Church in the shallow valley below. Cross to the church where a stile gives access to the little burial ground.

This church was built in the early 18th century by local people, but is now used only occasionally. It is one of the most isolated churches in England, in a superb setting.

From the church follow the path, right, up to Place Farm, going past the farmhouse and along the waymarked path (please keep to the path) up to Shaws. This timber-clad house was formerly Garsdale Youth Hostel and before that the home of Scott Macfie, a writer on gypsy lore who is buried in Lunds churchyard. Go through the gate to the right, and up the steps. Take a couple of minutes to investigate the splendid waterfall at the top of the steps. Walk along the grassy path which bears right uphill to a stile in the wall corner. Turn left onto the High Way.

Until 1825 this was the main road

between Hawes and Kirkby Stephen, for horse, foot and even carriage traffic, but particularily for the trains of pack-horses which once carried produce in large quantities around the Dales. Several of the old farms along this track were therefore once on a busy road, with some offering overnight accommodation for passing travellers. All are now isolated ruins. It was this route that Lady Anne took in a lumbering coach, accompanied by a train of retainers.

Follow this old road which offers both easy walking and fine views across the head of Wensleydale, soon passing an old farm — High Hall — by a small waterfall. Where the track leaves the walls and crosses open pasture, steer directly towards the farm and clump of trees ahead at Hell Gill, where a gateway leads to a bridge over a deep, narrow ravine.

Hell Gill Beck is both the source of the River Eden and the boundary between North Yorkshire and Cumbria. The stream encountered just a couple of hundred yards previously was the source of the Ure from Ure Heads heading for the North Sea. The River Eden, on the other hand, flows away towards the Solway Firth and the Irish Sea - the very watershed of England.

Follow what is now a superb, green way crossing the shoulder of the fell. This finally bears diagonally down between tussocky grass on a track which gradually descends to join the road at Thrang. Turn right along the road for a few yards, but at the next gate on the left, follow the track to the river at Thrang Bridge.

The path now follows the riverside, crossing an awkward stile in the wall corner and continuing to Mallerstang Farm. Go through the farm along the farm track; as this swings towards the river, cross the pasture on the left to a stile in the wall leading into a wood.

This becomes a lovely riverside and woodland path to Shoregill, a group of farms and cottages. Go through here, the path bearing right past the last cottages through a field gate and onto a sunken lane. Where this peters out, keep in the same direction through a series of stiles and gates.

Pathfinding is a little awkward around Moss Gill: cross the wall by the beck, keeping the wood on your left, over Riggs Gill beck, up to the barn, through the gate behind, along the fence to cross a beck and above a wood. Then go through a long field above the riverside. A stile leads onto riverside pasture, opposite the ruins of Pendragon Castle, at the end of which is a stile by Castle Bridge.

Legend has it that King Arthur was born at the castle, Uther Pendragon being his father's name, and the site may have Celtic origins. The ruins date from Norman times, and the castle was in the ownership of important local families, including the Viponts and the Cliffords throughout the Middle Ages. The last person to restore and inhabit it was Lady Anne Clifford.

From Pendragon Castle follow the lane as it swings back to the river. As it bends left, go through a gate on the right which leads to the track by Birkett Common. This is a fine stretch of open fellside, often grazed by semi-wild ponies. After just over a half-mile, at a junction of tracks, take the left fork which follows the fell round, soon going close by the river again.

Where it becomes a tarmaced way below Croop House, your way is through the gate on the right, past Lammerside Castle — another impressive ruin of a fortified medieval house or castle. The bridleway is marked by a series of field gates, the first behind the castle, the second in the next field but diagonally right, then keeping more or less the same direction into a long field by the river, emerging onto a farm track

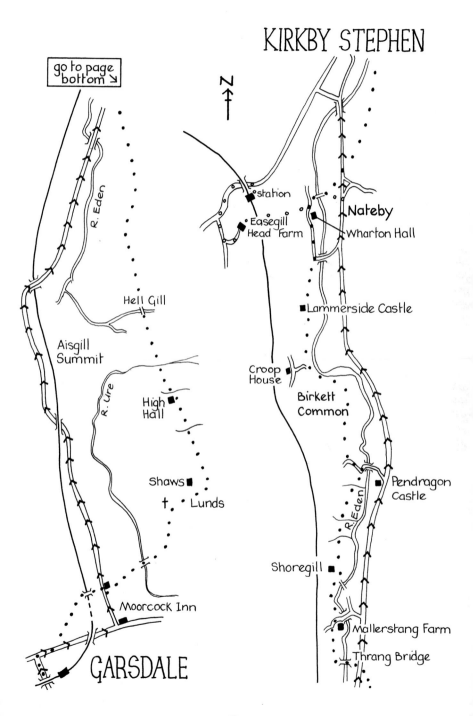

KIRKBY STEPHEN

go to page
bottom ↘

N ↑

R. Eden

station

Easegill
Head Farm

Nateby

Wharton Hall

Hell Gill

Lammerside Castle

Aisgill
Summit

R. Ure

Croop
House

High
Hall

Birkett
Common

Shaws
† Lunds

Pendragon
Castle

R. Eden

Shoregill

Moorcock Inn

Mallerstang Farm

Thrang Bridge

GARSDALE

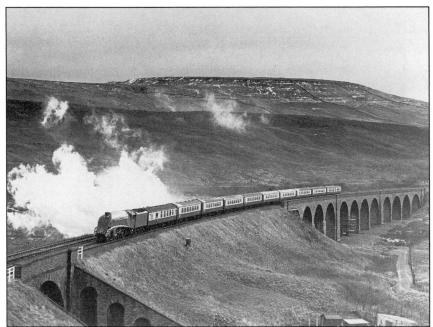

*Above: Sir Nigel Gresley hauls a Pullman special north out of Garsdale across Dandry Mire viaduct. **Below:** Slightly further north, is the line's summit at Aisgill, from where the fine panorama of the Eden Valley opens out, with Wild Boar Fell on the left and Mallerstang Edge on the right. Lady Anne Clifford's Way follows the flanks of the escarpment on the right. The freight train is something never seen on the S & C nowadays.*

The way up to Lady Anne Clifford's Way passes some picturesque waterfalls.

to Wharton Hall. This is a fine example of a house fortified against the frequent Scottish raids; it dates from the 14th century with much surviving medieval and Tudor fabric, and is still a home and working farm.

The quickest way from Wharton to Kirkby Stephen station is to continue for 200 yards along the farm drive before turning sharp left, by an ancient oak, and up the hillside. A stile in the wall leads to a path up sloping pasture to a gate, then a tunnel under the railway to Easegill Head farm. To reach the station, go right along the A683 and A685 roads. There is an occasional minibus service between Kirkby Stephen and its station; otherwise it's almost an hour's walk.

For Kirkby Stephen town, bear right just beyond Wharton Hall for the path which slopes down to the riverside. You now have a choice of paths bearing right into Nateby village (shop and pub), from where a bridleway leads directly into the town.

Kirkby Stephen is a handsome old market town at the northern end of the bleak yet beautiful Mallerstang valley. Granted its market charter in 1351, the town used to host a number of major fairs and markets, such as the Couper Day horse fair and the St Luke's sheep fair. To cater for this trade, and for the stage-coach travellers for whom Kirkby Stephen was a welcome halt, the town once boasted a total of seventeen pubs and inns.

Bull-baiting was a common sight in the market square, until the practice was outlawed in 1814. Today there is a weekly market (Mondays) and regular sheep sales, but churches now outnumber the pubs!

Next to the cobbled market square are cloisters, where the butter market used to be held. The market rules are still displayed here. Through the cloisters you will find the parish church; because of its size it is often referred to as the Cathedral of the Dales. Parts of the church date from the 13th century, though the tower is 16th century.

There is a recently restored Shambles (an old name for a butcher's shop) and a spinning gallery; the latter is a reminder of when hand spinning and knitting comprised an important cottage industry in this area. The Youth Hostel on the long Main Street is actually a converted Methodist Chapel, and the chapel balcony has been retained as an elevated common room.

● **CYCLE TRAIL:** Cyclists take a similar route to walkers along this section from Garsdale station to Kirkby Stephen station — but along the valley bottom of Mallerstang rather than the High Way of Lady Anne Clifford.

Pass Garsdale station, at the northern end of the Coal Road from Dentdale, and turn right along the A684 — the principal east-west route through the Yorkshire Dales National Park. At this point you join the Cumbria Cycle Way, and stay with it all the way to Glassonby. So at every fork and junction you will be guided by little brown signs featuring "Cumbria" and a little cycle logo.

Turn left along the B6259 immediately before the Moorcock Inn; this is the road you follow right up to Kirkby Stephen. About two miles past the pub, keep a look-out for a couple of waterfalls. Hell Gill Force, 500 yards to the right of the road, tumbles over a rocky outcrop in spectacular fashion. The other waterfall is closer to the road, in a little disused quarry on the left.

Half a mile past the little village of Outhgill, is the ruined stump of Pendragon Castle. As the railway bears off to the left towards Kirkby Stephen station, the road leads into the town itself. ❑

The ruins of Pendragon Castle, legendary birthplace of King Arthur. The owner is engaged on a long-term project, under the watchful eye of English Heritage, to consolidate the remains.

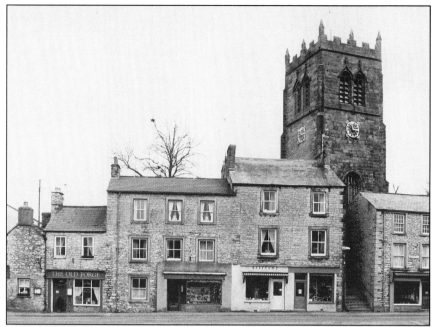

A variety of roof lines along the main street of Kirkby Stephen, with the parish church behind.

Blue faced Leicester tups are often crossed with Swaledale ewes to produce mule fat lambs.

Kirkby Stephen to Appleby

A 15-mile (27 km) walk from one characterful old market town to another, taking in some interesting railway architecture and finishing with a delightful walk along the River Eden.

TO begin this section of the route, walk south down the main street of Kirkby Steven, in the direction of Kendal. Take one of the many right turns, before you leave the village, to join a little lane that runs at the back of — and parallel to — the main road. This thoroughfare runs along the backs of houses; once you leave the houses behind, it narrows and becomes an unmade track called Croglam Lane. Very soon you will see ancient earthworks on your left; these are the unexcavated remains of a prehistoric hill fort.

Carry along the track to arrive at Greenriggs Farm. Go through a gate into the farmyard (yes, it's a right of way); turn right here and then almost immediately left — look out for the "footpath" signs — to go through what was once a short tunnel beneath the old Darlington-Tebay railway line. Now, with the removal of the rails, it is open to the sky.

Walk up a hill and through a gate. Look out for the waymarking here — "C to C" — and for a good deal of this section of the walk. Yes, we are joining the famous Coast to Coast walk, a long-distance route initiated by Alfred Wainwright, that guides energetic hikers from St Bees in Cumbria to Robin Hood's Bay in Yorkshire. For the next few miles we share this route.

Keep walking uphill, over a stile, into open fields. The path hereabouts is indistinct; when in doubt just keep straight ahead. After a miniature limestone outcrop take another stile, and bear slightly left to cross beneath the Settle-Carlisle line via a tunnel. Walk straight ahead, keeping a barn and walled enclosure to your right. Bear slightly right after the barn to reach a gate and minor road.

Turn left along the road for 150 yards, and then right along an even lesser road (with grass growing in the middle!) which is signposted "Smardale". Follow this road for just 100 yards, take a ladder stile on the left, and walk uphill onto Smardale Fell. After another 100 yards, make a slight detour to your left to find an old limekiln.

These sturdy structures were constructed, generally in the 18th century, wherever limestone was easy to quarry. They are typically squat, square and themselves constructed of limestone, with an arched opening at the front. Almost invariably they were built into the side of a slope.

Limestone had many uses, particularly building, walling and, after firing, enriching the land. The kilns were used for burning it and converting it to a fine powder suitable for mortar or sweetening acid soil. The raw materials for this process were close at hand, in the form of the plentiful limestone escarpments, and peat or locally mined coal as sources of fuel. Layers of limestone and fuel

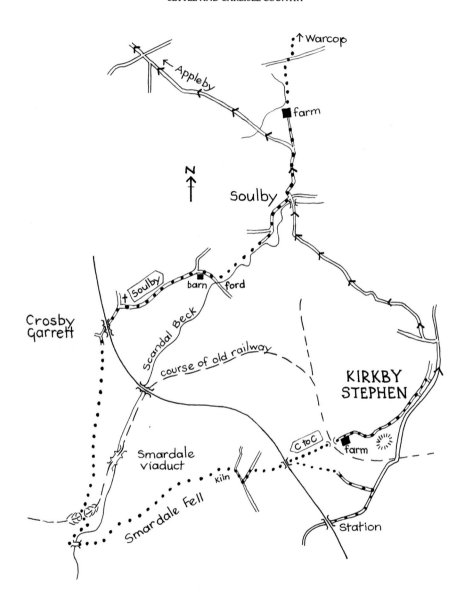

were fed into the kilns from the top, left to burn slowly and the powdered lime would later be removed from the hole at the bottom.

These small kilns were built and used by farmers to provide lime for their own soil. They were never intended to be run on commercial lines, and all are now obsolete. For large-scale production there were limestone quarries and industrial-sized kilns. And you'll see examples of these in a very short while on this section of the walk.

While the small kilns are now surplus

to farming requirements, there is actually more limestone being taken today than ever before. The Yorkshire Dales National Park, for example, has a grand total of eight limestone quarries within its boundaries, most of which are over-prominent eyesores. And the top layers of many of the limestone pavements have been removed for the dubious purpose of providing ornamental stone for walls and rockeries.

Rejoin the path and continue to climb, keeping the field wall to your right. At the top, bear slightly left to make the descent. Head towards a prominent clump of trees on the first horizon. When you meet a wall, follow it uphill past the trees. Follow the wall downhill from here, and cross a ladder stile. Look to your right and get your first glimpse of a river gorge; you'll be seeing a good deal more of it as the walk progresses. On the opposite side of the river there is, as promised, an old limestone quarry, with a pair of industrial-sized limekilns.

Cross a stile and take an engineered sunken track down to Smardale Bridge, which spans the delightfully-named Scandal Beck. If you look at the field walls in the vicinity you will see the way that the red sandstone is gradually taking over from the limestone; this mixture of colour gives the walls a pleasantly variegated appearance.

Go over the bridge, through a gate and turn immediately to the right. Take the distinct path that rises up and follows the top of a limestone escarpment. The path follows — though at a higher level — the course of the beck to your right. On the left you will see the old Tebay railway line, soon to be crossed on a stone footbridge as the line goes into a cutting.

Keep right over the bridge, past a solitary building. Once it was faced with slates, but now it is abandoned and the slates that remain clatter in the wind. Cross a stile and climb up to the right, away from the line, to follow a field wall. Continue along the top of the outcrop, getting a good view into the steep-sided valley below.

You will see lines of limestone outcrops on the far side of the gorge and, soon, get a bird's-eye view of the old Smardale viaduct, which carries the old railway line obliquely from one side of the valley to the other. This viaduct was saved from demolition following a recent public enquiry, but its condition continues to cause concern. On the opposite side of the valley the railway line follows the steep incline on a ledge, and through a nature reserve. In front of you, beyond the wooded valley, is the other, newer, Smardale viaduct, which carries the Settle-Carlisle railway. It is, at 130ft, the tallest viaduct on the line.

Having looked at Smardale viaduct, head slightly left and away from the gorge. Climb uphill to join a farm track which has recently been resurfaced. Follow it to the right; it leads unerringly down into Crosby Garrett. Two hundred yards before entering the village, you will find on your right a couple more limekilns, almost hidden in a dip.

Crosby Garrett is almost dwarfed by its railway viaduct; nevertheless the village has enough interesting features to make you halt awhile. You enter it, appropriately enough, through one arch of the viaduct. Notice the fords and the many little footbridges spanning the stream that runs between the houses.

The church of St Andrew sits in splendid isolation on top of a hill at the far end of the village. Its elevated position makes the church seem larger than it actually is. However, it makes up in character what it lacks in size. You will know if the church is open for visitors: there will be a notice to this effect hanging on the churchyard gate.

A church has stood on this hill for at least a thousand years. The name "Crosby" indicates that this was a mis-

sion station before the church was built, with a cross planted on the hill for preaching purposes. The hill is called Arklow, which means a place of sacrifice. So the site may predate Christianity altogether and be a spot where pagan ceremonies were held.

Parts of the church date back to the tenth century, though most of the nave is Saxon. The asymmetrical shape of the nave is due to it having been enlarged in Norman times. This addition meant that many people in the congregation would no longer have been able to see the altar, so a "squint hole" was knocked through the offending wall.

The bell-tower was rebuilt in 1874, a date which implies a connection with the building of the Settle-Carlisle line and, specifically, the raising of Crosby Garrett's 50ft high viaduct. Given the influx of building labourers for this major engineering undertaking, this was probably the busiest era in the long history of this delightful little church.

Leave Crosby Garrett on the road that passes the church, signposted "Soulby". As the road bears left, after about half a mile, bear right by a barn along an even more minor road, which has grass growing along the middle. Follow it down to a little beck — this is Scandal Beck once more — where you'll find a ford and a wooden footbridge. Ignore these, however, and take instead a little gate on the left, just 20 yards before the beck.

Follow the beck until you reach a farm; there is a right of way through the farmyard and then along a track which takes you into Soulby. The village sits astride a bend in the river, which is crossed by a sandstone bridge. There is a village green so extensive that you might almost call it a meadow. Soulby is nothing like some of the cramped little villages of the Yorkshire Dales, met earlier in the walk. Here the houses are spread out with room to spare.

Walk to the crossroads in the middle of the village, and turn left by a couple of long-forgotten petrol pumps; the signpost indicates "Appleby".

Two hundred yards out of the village, take a track to the right, as the road bears left. Follow the track to a farm; walk unhesitatingly into the farmyard and out the other side onto a gated track. After the second gate, leave the track and bear left to follow the beck for a short way.

Soon the beck goes left and flows beneath a little stone bridge. But you carry straight on, and aim for a dark grey barn that appears prominently ahead. Cross some boggy pasture, go over a stile and pass just to the left of the barn. Go downhill to join a very minor road; go right for 100 yards, then left over a little bridge fashioned from railway sleepers. Go through a gate, and straight across a field, making for a small wood ahead.

When you are just 100 yards from the right-hand corner of the wood, you'll come up against a fence that bars your way. So turn right here and accompany the fence until you see a couple of farms to the left. Go between the buildings and carry straight on to join a farm track. Bear uphill along the track, which is soon bordered by hedgerows. At the top there are good views to your right — over the river and to the fells beyond.

The track descends towards the river; ignore a track branching off left. Keep straight on, over a cattle grid, as the track narrows and follows the river. Shame on whoever dumped an old car on the opposite bank. Through a little iron gate, the track becomes a pleasant footpath that takes you through trees, then meadowland, to arrive at Warcop Bridge.

Left: The old Smardale railway viaduct, near Crosby Garrett, and the meandering course of Scardale Beck.

Cross the bridge only if you want to take a look at Warcop village — its houses straggling along a winding road, and clustered round little greens.

To continue the walk, don't cross the bridge. Turn left along the road, instead, for 50 yards, and take a track to the right, following the river, waymarked "Blacksyke". This track soon forks; the right fork is a private road to Langford Farm, so bear left here. Walk uphill to where the track makes a sharp left-hand turn; carry straight ahead on a grassy, enclosed track.

Bear left through a gate and follow the track as it accompanies the edge of a field. When the track forks yet again, take the right-hand track through a field gate. Climb up to a ridge, and get a panoramic view down the valley to your left. On the descent, go through a couple of gates to arrive just to the right of the Blacksyke farm buildings.

Don't cross the little river bridge nearby, but take a track to another farm close by, keeping the river to your right. Go through the farmyard; immediately afterwards there is a path to the right that follows the edge of a wood. Follow this pleasant woodland path uphill, go through a gate and carry

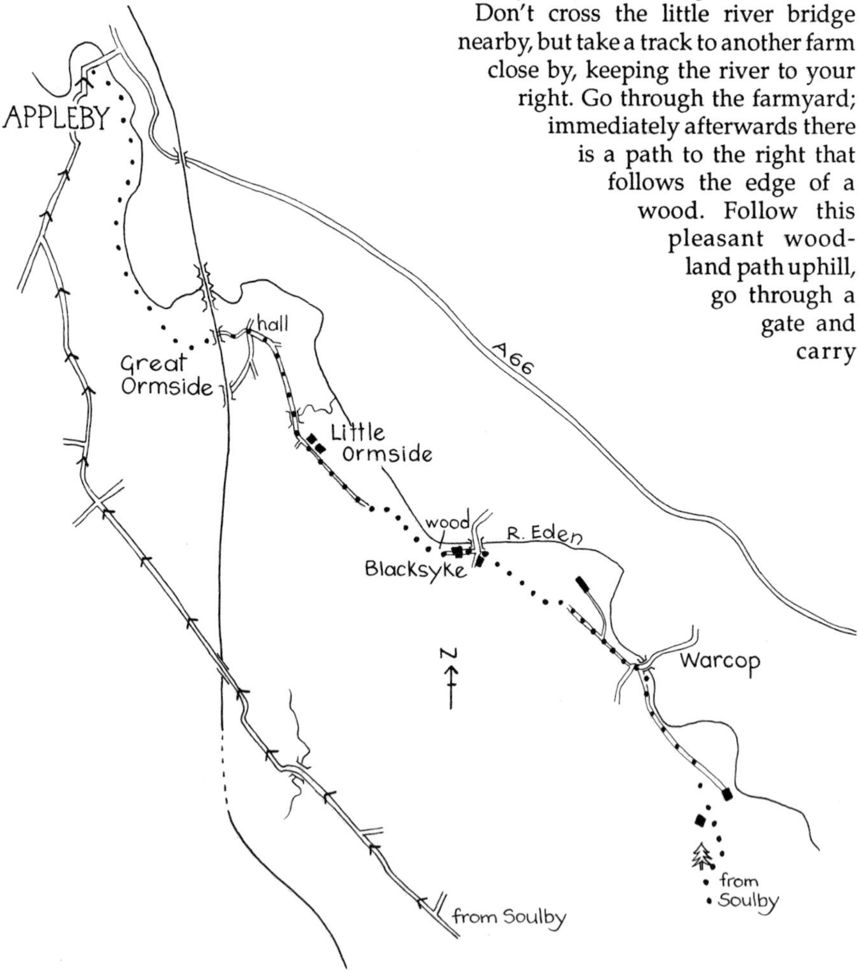

APPLEBY

hall

Great
Ormside

Little
Ormside

wood

R. Eden

Blacksyke

A 66

Warcop

N ↑

from
Soulby

from Soulby

straight on to accompany a fence along the edge of a field.

When the line of trees fizzles out, you should get some good views down the valley to your right, and the A66 trunk road from Appleby to Brough. Beyond the road are bleak and brooding fells, which stretch many inhospitable miles to the north and east. They have been commandeered by the Ministry of Defence for military manoeuvres.

Your path soon becomes a well-defined farm track; follow it for about half a mile to pass on your right the couple of farms that comprise Little Ormside. Notice the rather artistic use of multi-coloured sheets of corrugated iron that give the barns the appearance of a patchwork quilt!

The track soon becomes a tarmaced road. The last building you see is a handsome barn on the right; notice the ramp to facilitate the unloading of carts. Follow the road into Great Ormside: it's "Great" only in comparsion with Little Ormside, but nonetheless worth a look around. With only one road in and out of the village, there is no through traffic to disturb its air of unhurried tranquility.

A prominent feature by the road junction is a sycamore tree surrounded by stone steps, which was the site of a regular cheese and butter market. The tree may have been planted after the original stone cross had been destroyed by Puritans during the Civil War. From here you can see Great Ormside's two buildings of distinction: Ormside Hall and St James' Church.

The hall was orginally a fortified pele tower, built in the 14th century, when border raids were an ever-present threat. The walls were seven feet thick, capable of withstanding a short siege. The hall, enlarged in the 16th century, is now a working farm.

Nearby is the church of St James, looking down on the village from a grassy knoll. Parts of the tower and nave date back to the 12th century, though the oak roof and many of the furnishings are 17th century. In the days of the border raids a lamp was kept lit in one of the church windows, to guide any traveller who might need sanctuary.

A number of interesting artifacts have been unearthed from the churchyard. The most important find to date has been an Anglo-Saxon cup, discovered in 1823 and donated to the Yorkshire Museum in York. It dates from about 800-850 AD, and shows a Celtic influence in its design and workmanship. A display in the church gives more information about the finds.

You can get a good view from the church of the Ormside viaduct nearby, which carries the Settle-Carlisle railway. This is the first of many crossings that the line will make of the River Eden.

Having looked round the village, make your way back to the crossroads. Between the tree with the steps round it, and adjacent farm buildings, is an enclosed track. Follow the track as it bends left, right and left again to go underneath the Settle-Carlisle railway line. Immediately afterwards the track bears right, but you carry straight on, over a ladder style. After a few more yards, bear left to continue along a broad, grassy enclosed way.

Walk downhill to an open field, where a yellow arrow will guide you to the right, down towards trees. Cross a tiny footbridge over an equally tiny stream, and negotiate a stile. Walk along a lovely path through a wooded ghyll. Cross a slightly larger stream (on a correspondingly larger bridge), and bear right up a steep path.

Take a stile at the top and carry on over another stile; now you have level walking with silver birch trees to your right. Soon, over the tree-tops, you will see the River Eden. The path descends gradually, and then more steeply, as a yellow arrow points you directly down to the riverside.

For the rest of this section of the walk, the path does not stray more than a few yards from the water's edge. It's a delightful way to end the day: strolling along the wooded banks of the Eden. There should be abundant bird-life at any season of the year — perhaps slate-grey herons standing perfectly still as they wait for fish, or moorhens skittering across the river, trailing their legs in the water. In summer, these woods are alive with the songs of warblers, and wagtails run daintily along the water's edge.

As you approach Appleby, you will see new houses on top of a bank to your right, and hear the rushing water of a wier close by. You walk in the shadow of a high sandstone wall, through a kissing gate and then left up a lane between high walls. Turn right when you meet a road at the top, and follow the wall to your right. As you'll soon discover for yourself, behind this wall is Appleby Castle.

As you round the wall you will find yourself at the top of Boroughgate, looking down into the town. Appleby is a delightful town that still keeps its essentially medieval layout, with the broad main street of Boroughgate leading down from the castle at the top to the parish church. To continue the walk, make your way up to the railway station. But if you have the time, why not investigate the many interesting corners of this historic town with the town trail on page 136.

● **CYCLE TRAIL:** From Kirkby Stephen,go north along the A685 towards Brough. Opposite the town church, take a road to the left, signposted to Crosby Garrett, and then, almost immediately, a road to the right, to Soulby. Look right to see, in the distance, the extensive fells that will be a prominent feature for much of your ride.

Go straight through the spacious village of Soulby; the walkers' route soon bears right, but you carry on along the road and, after about three miles, over the Settle-Carlisle line. A couple of miles further on, you join the B6260. Bear right here to descend into Appleby.   ❏

Great Ormside, with the fortified hall to the right, and the old sycamore tree — once the site of a butter market — in the foreground..

Appleby to Langwathby

A 13-mile (20km)walk which takes you through handsome fell-side villages, crossing the Pennine Way, and following the route of a Roman road.The day ends a Langwathby, on the River Eden.

WHETHER you have stayed in Appleby, or just arrived on the train, the station makes a convenient beginning for this section of the route. (If you arrived on a northbound train, you can leave by the nearest exit. If you arrived on a southbound train then you should cross over the footbridge.)

Follow a little path from the station to the road, and turn right along it. Walk up the hill and over a level crossing. This is the Warcop line which, until recently, carried munitions to the Ministry of Defence ranges at Warcop. The line is all that remains of the old North Eastern railway line from Darlington to Penrith. British Rail has been trying to find a buyer to transform it into an enthusiasts' railway.

After the level crossing, bear left onto a footpath waymarked "Hungriggs Lane". Climb a ladder stile and cross, with care, the busy dual carriageway; then up steps, over a stile, across another road and another stile, to go straight ahead across a field.

Negotiate a kissing gate, and turn right along a narrow road. After a few yards, go through a gate and turn immediately left down a pleasant enclosed path between fields. After a stile, bear right across a field to reach another stile at the far end. Walk along a field edge for a few yards then take a stile on the left into a conifer wood. Take a path downhill, following the wood's left edge.

Having crossed a small stream, head off left on a path that runs roughly parallel to the stream. Follow the stream through pleasant open pasture, keeping to the left of a conifer wood. Follow the edge of the wood to the right, through a gate and over a little bridge. Bear right along a well-defined path: well-defined by tractor wheels at any rate. Note the old saw mill on your right, now in a rather dilapidated state.

Enter the wood — a scene of devastation (at the time of writing) as the trees are being felled in great numbers. The ground has been churned up by tractor wheels, so no pathway is visible. Just head straight up the wood, and down the other side. Take the most direct route towards the nearest patch of open fields, while trying to avoid the boggy bits. Hopefully, the tree-felling will now be complete, and the path correspondingly clearer.

Bear slightly right up the field to reach the right-hand corner of a spur of the wood. Keeping the wood to your left, cross a makeshift stile. Follow a wall; when it falls away to the left, walk down to a stile and over a bridge across a beck. Bear right around a hillock and then, keeping straight ahead, negotiate a series of stiles, gates and ill-defined field paths. Keep your OS map handy here, in case of indecision.

You will eventually emerge from open fields by a handsome white farmhouse

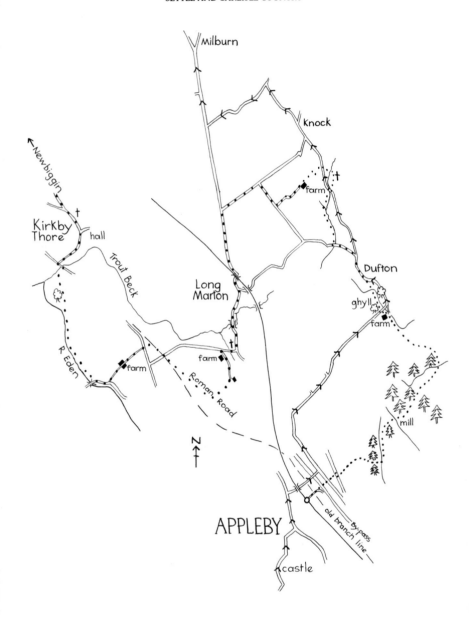

with windows and mouldings picked out in red. Join a farm track; then, after a few yards, branch left over a stile, and go through a field to a road. Turn left here for a few yards, then right, through a wooded ghyll or small ravine. The path is waymarked "Ghyll and Dufton".

Until the Woodland Trust took it over, the Ghyll belonged to the Lord of the Manor. The Trust has been operating a replanting scheme here, with more than 3,000 trees being planted in recent years. Wild flowers, too, make a splash of colour in the spring and summer.

Take a look at the sandstone cliffs rising up to your left, and notice the way that small trees cling precariously to its face and ledges. Walk along this pleasant path through woodland, following a beck. Cross a wooden footbridge and take a track uphill into the village of Dufton.

The name Dufton is Anglo-Saxon and means "a farmstead where doves are reared". The village's layout is Anglo-Saxon too, with houses and farms grouped around a spacious village green. This arrangement offered some defence against raiders from the north, and also against the Helm: a wild north-easterly wind that can roll down with some ferocity from the heights of Cross Fell.

The area had been a thriving centre for the lead-mining industry, until the bottom fell out of the market towards the end of the last century. The village was largely built, in fact, by the London Lead Company, a Quaker-owned concern, to house the miners who worked the seams and levels driven deep into the surrounding fells.

To the north-east of Dufton are some of the highest fells in the Pennines; Cross Fell is 2,930 feet high, and the dramatic ravine of High Cup Gill is just a steady ramble away. You may see other ramblers in the area, because the Pennine Way passes both these landmarks and takes in Dufton too. To cater for the needs of foot-weary hikers there is a Youth Hostel in the village.

The name of the Stag Inn, next to the green, recalls a time when deer roamed the forests around Dufton. William Rufus, who conquered the north and built the castles of Appleby and Brough, was fond of stag-hunting here.

The village of Dufton, with its splendid water fountain, sits right at the edge of the fells; Dufton Pike is to the left.

Walk through the village; just after the last house, the road forks. Take the left fork, signposted "Long Marton and Penrith". After 200 yards, cross a river and take a field path to the right, way-marked "St Cuthberts Church". Walk on the low path, to keep the river company.

Negotiate a couple of stiles close together; the path still accompanies the river, but at a higher level. A wooden bridge can be seen; keep left of it and take a gate ahead, waymarked with a blue arrow. Keep your eyes open and you might see a dipper on this stretch of the river. Go through a gate and turn right as you reach a road. Turn left soon, on a track that leads straight to St Cuthbert's Church.

Legend has it that the church was built by monks from Lindisfarne, who fled from the Vikings in 875 AD with the body of St Cuthbert. There has long been a church on this site, though the present building dates only from 1784.

After looking at the church, cross the graveyard; it is a permissive path and there's a gate at the far side that leads into a field. There is a painted yellow arrow here to guide your way, and there are others at regular intervals during the next section of the walk.

Head across a field to where wall and beck meet, and cross the stile. Follow the beck upstream and then cross it on a footbridge. Leave the beck and bear right to follow a fence and reach a road. Bear to the right along the road. Ahead of you are the symmetrical contours of Knock Pike; the fell to your right is Dufton Pike.

The first house you encounter is called "Heater" — actually a dialect name for a triangular piece of land. Turn sharp left directly behind the house, to join an enclosed path between fields. Where this track joins another, at a T-junction of paths, turn right. After a few yards go through a gate on the left, and take a field path to the farm ahead. Pass to the right of the farmhouse. At some time in the past this building was kitted out — somewhat incongruously — with a porch and bow windows that would be more fitting in suburbia than in rural Cumbria.

Follow the farm track to a road, and turn right here. Follow the road to a T-junction, turn left and continue downhill. Go left again at another T-junction, and walk past the now disused railway station into the village of Long Marton.

As well as a modern housing estate, there are many fine old houses in the centre of the village, some bearing date-stones which authenticate their age. One example bears the inscription: "John Bellas and Margraef his wife, 1740". This is a departure from the more common style of indicating names merely by initials. When these initials are arranged in a triangular shape, the top one is the initial of the family surname, while the lower two initials signify the pair of Christian names. Personalising houses in this way seems to be an interesting tradition. Do we have as much pride in the houses we are building today?

Walk straight through the village, over the bridge across Trout Beck, and up to the church a little way from the village it serves. Features of interest include little scenes carved in relief, which can be found over the south and west doorways. One is carved with a dragon, merman, club and cross. The other has quaint figures of a dragon and a winged ox in a boat.

Turn right immediately after the church, onto a road signposted "Penrith". After about 200 yards go left along a cement track, waymarked to "Croft Ends and Crackenthorpe". Pass a farm; just a few yards before you reach another farm (Far Broome), go right through a field gate — waymarked with a yellow arrow. Walk uphill, keeping close to the hedgerow on your right. Go through a gate, and over a stile to find yourself on the ruler-straight green track that you will not be surprised to learn is an old Roman road.

Turn right along it. This section of roadway has not been incorporated into the fields to either side; it is still a broad thoroughfare used by walkers and horse-riders. An abandoned railway line soon approaches and then runs parallel to your route. After about a mile of walking the Roman road, you meet a more modern highway. Cross it and bear slightly left to follow another ruler-straight route: the railway track running along an embankment.

Just beyond a track-side bungalow, take a ladder stile (made, unusually, of concrete) to the left and walk across the field to a gate. Cross the busy main road (the A66) and go a few yards to the right to pick up a farm track on your left, signposted to "Redlands Bank Farm". Walk straight into the farmyard and out the other side. Follow the track until you meet both a road and the river Eden close to a caravan site.

Go right along the road to accompany the river. A few yards before a handsome two-arch river bridge, take a little stile in the wall to your right. Carry on walking by the riverside; soon you will see houses in the distance, indicating the village of Kirkby Thore. Follow the river until you reach a small copse; bear right here, through a gate, and follow the edge of the copse. Soon you join a farm track which bears right and takes you through another farmyard into Kirkby Thore, just where the main road crosses Trout Beck.

Turn right immediately past the pub and walk through the village. Turn left on the road signposted "Newbiggin". Have you ever wondered why it is that so many villages — in these parts and elsewhere — bear this name? The answer is simple: biggin means building.

As you leave the village, you may see smoke rising from a chimney away to your right. It emanates from the Kirkby Thore gypsum mine. Keep walking; you'll see the Settle-Carlisle line coming ever closer on your right. Cross the road on a bridge close to the Newbiggin gypsum mine on the left. Walk into Newbiggin and then straight on at the crossroads, signposted "Blencarn and Culgaith". Newbiggin Hall is immediately to your right, as is the church.

Cross the bridge and follow the road as it climbs. Where it bends sharply to the right, take a track to the left, way-marked "Culgaith Village". The track climbs, bears right and ends in a field. Take a stile and walk ahead, keeping to the right edge of the field. You begin to get extensive views to your right. The hills you can see are, from left to right, Cross Fell, Knock Pike, Dufton Pike, Murton Pike and Roman Fell.

After the second stile, walk round the edge of the field towards a stile at the far left corner. Join a track until you meet a road; turn right along it into Culgaith. After the village post office, take a cobbled path to the right, waymarked "Stainsgills Road End". Pass by a delightful Wesleyan Methodist chapel, and go over a stepped stile. Walk along the edge of a field, keeping the hedge to your left. Cross another stile and then go through a gate — the hedge now being on your right — to reach a road. Take a road ahead signposted "Moorside and Stainsgills". It is marked as a cul-de-sac, but that only applies to cars.

Go past a few houses, as the road deteriorates into an unmade track. It bears right and then left in front of a farm; take a track here which bears to the right, towards a wood. As you reach the wood, go through a gate and turn left along a wooded track. When you leave the woodland, the path meanders pleasantly between walls and birch trees. Meet a road, turn left along it and

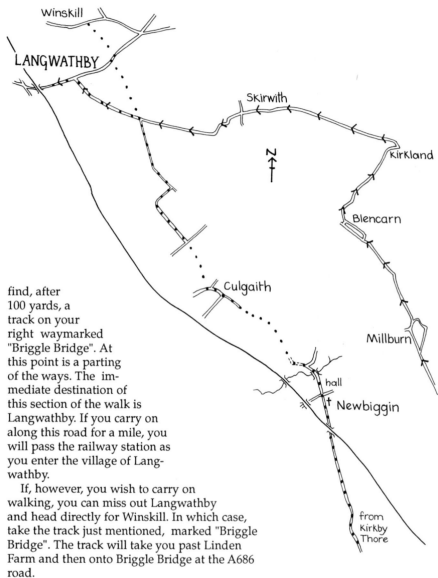

find, after
100 yards, a
track on your
right waymarked
"Briggle Bridge". At
this point is a parting
of the ways. The im-
mediate destination of
this section of the walk is
Langwathby. If you carry on
along this road for a mile, you
will pass the railway station as
you enter the village of Langwathby.

If, however, you wish to carry on
walking, you can miss out Langwathby
and head directly for Winskill. In which case,
take the track just mentioned, marked "Briggle
Bridge". The track will take you past Linden
Farm and then onto Briggle Bridge at the A686
road.

Turn right along the road. After about 200 yards,
take a wall stile on the left, waymarked "Winskill and
Hunsonby". Follow the field path into the village of
Winskill.

● **CYCLE TRAIL:** From the centre of Appleby, climb up
towards the station and past it. Go over the new by-pass too,
and then, at a T-junction, bear left on a road signposted to

The village of Langwathby is the destination for this section of the walk.

"Dufton and Knock". There is a good downill gradient into Dufton; you will see signs indicating the Pennine Way bearing off to your right.

Pass St Cuthbert's church as you continue on to Knock. Cycle straight through the village, noticing the conical shape of Knock Fell to your right.

Turn right when you meet a T-junction, to arrive shortly in in the village of Milburn, whose layout — with houses clustered round an extensive village green — once gave protection against Border raids.

After crossing the delightfully-named Crowdundle Beck, you reach Blencarn; from here you turn right towards Kirkland, the closest village to the mass off Cross Fell you see ahead. Carry on to Skirwith, pleasant collection of houses grouped either side of a ghyll, and then into Langwathby. ❏

Langwathby to Armathwaite

A 13-mile (20km) walk that begins with an ancient stone circle and follows the River Eden to Lacy's Caves. There are fine riverside rambles to enjoy at the Nunnery Walks.

LANGWATHBY is another Eden village whose *by* suffix indicates Viking origins. Its name means "settlement by a long ford". Cottages and farmhouses cluster round the village green of Langwathby where a Maypole — still in use each year — is to be found.

The Bailey Bridge over the river carries the Penrith road, and was built in 1968 to replace a sandstone bridge that had been swept away by floods. The new bridge was meant to be merely a stop-gap measure, though it has earned an entry in the Guinness Book of Records as the longest lasting "temporary" bridge in the country.

To begin this section of the walk, leave the railway station and turn left along the road for 100 yards. Then turn right at crossroads, signposted "Feed Mill". Take first road to right, again signed "feed mill", and go under the railway. Pass the busy mill buildings.

When the road makes a sharp right turn, go left along a farm track waymarked "Winskill & Hunsonby". After 50 yards take another track to the right. After 250 yards take a field path to the left, waymarked "Winskill". Follow the wall to your left until you reach a wooden footbridge over Briggle Beck. Go through a beck-side copse, up through a field, and via a gate. Turn right along the road to arrive in Winskill.

There are some pleasant cottages in the village, plus a corrugated-iron building which a sign informs is "The Sons of Temperance Room". After 100 yards turn left up a track between houses, and by a phonebox. The path may look private, but it's not. Walk past a house, and through a kissing gate. Follow the edge of a field to another house and more kissing gates until you reach a road. Cross the road and bear slightly right, down a grassy path. Cross a liitle beck on an arched bridge. Follow the path — it may be a bit boggy after rain — to arrive in the village of Hunsonby.

At the road turn left onto the village green. After a few yards, turn left again, along an unmade track that runs between a house and an open-sided barn.

Follow this track. Again, it may be boggy after rain. After half a mile the track narrows to a footpath. Go through a gate into open fields, then downhill and over a tiny stream. Climb up a hill, bearing left at the top to reach a gate at the far left end of the field. Join a farm track and skirt houses to reach a road. Left is to the village of Little Salkeld; we'll visit it later. But for now, turn right instead to visit a fascinating relic.

After nearly half a mile turn left at a minor road, signposted "Long Meg and Druids Circle". Follow the road; you can't miss the stone circle — Long Meg and her Daughters — since the road runs smack through the middle of it!

The stone circle (actually an oval) is 300 ft across, and is made up of 66 stones.

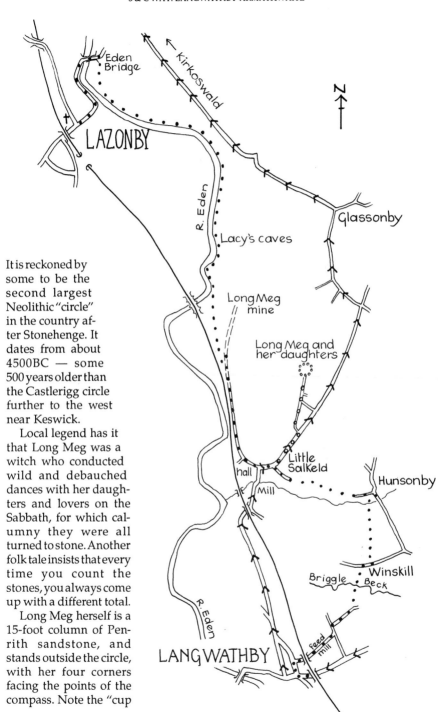

It is reckoned by some to be the second largest Neolithic "circle" in the country after Stonehenge. It dates from about 4500BC — some 500 years older than the Castlerigg circle further to the west near Keswick.

Local legend has it that Long Meg was a witch who conducted wild and debauched dances with her daughters and lovers on the Sabbath, for which calumny they were all turned to stone. Another folk tale insists that every time you count the stones, you always come up with a different total.

Long Meg herself is a 15-foot column of Penrith sandstone, and stands outside the circle, with her four corners facing the points of the compass. Note the "cup and ring" markings on the side of the stone; these are later additions. Similar markings overseas are held to point to a "pan-European" Bronze Age culture hundreds of years older than might originally have been thought. The "daughters" are of much harder sandstone, and would appear to have been transported from further afield.

The purpose of these stones is open to conjecture. However, the circle is clearly geared to the solar calendar: Long Meg's shadow runs straight up the circle's central axis on midwinter's day, and there are signs of ley lines stretching up the fell beyond.

Having soaked up the atmosphere of this ancient site, retrace your steps to arrive at Little Salkeld, its houses grouped around a triangular green. The village used to be a stopping station on the Settle-Carlisle line, but now the trains rush straight by.

Take a look, perhaps, at the old mill by the river. It is one of the few watermills in the country still producing stoneground flour by water power.

Entering the village from Long Meg, the through road bears left. Take the right fork, keeping Salkeld Hall on your left. The road is a cul-de-sac, but this only applies to motor traffic. The road soon forks again; the left fork goes under the railway, but you take the right fork waymarked "Long Meg, Lacey Caves & Dale Raven". It also says "private road", but it's not private to pedestrians.

The track runs close by (and parallel to) the railway line. On the far side of the line is the River Eden; beyond that is the village of Great Salkeld with its fortified church. You pass a footbridge over the railway, then a signal-box, then sidings. Pass two ruined sandstone buildings to reach a gate across the track and a sign saying "Long Meg, Keep Out".

Long Meg here refers not to the stone circle but to the former British Gypsum mine which closed in 1973. It has had a

chequered history, being closed and reopened on a number of occasions during the previous century — reflecting the changing price of, and demand for, the two main products. These were gypsum for plaster products (and more recently as an additive to "non-wholemeal" white bread) and anhydrite for making sulphuric acid and explosives.

Bear left here on a path way-marked "Lacey Caves & Dale Raven". After a few yards turn sharp left. Pass an electricity sub-station station, then bear sharp right on a fenced-in path. The main railway line swings away to the left, and a viaduct carries it over the river. It was four years in the making, and four of the viaduct's seven pillars are anchored beneath the waters of the Eden.

The River Eden is quite turbulent here. On the opposite bank of the river is an old corn mill which was powered by river water. The path descends through woodland down to the river. There are numerous old workings — the remains of mines and plaster works. The path you are following was once used by the miners from Kirkoswald going to and from work. Your route was also a mine tramway; in places you can see the remains of the rails.

For centuries this spot was one of the main river crossings. The first bridge was a pack-horse bridge, guarded by a small fort at its western end. Many other bridges were erected after that, though all succumbed to the destructive power of flood waters.

If you look ahead you will see caves carved out of a sandstone cliff directly above the river. When you reach the cliff itself, bear left on a permissive path carved out of the sandstone. Watch your feet here; the path may be slippery and it's a steep drop down to the river. Round a corner to find five arched and connecting chambers hewn out of the sandstone; these are Lacy's Caves.

The five connecting chambers of Lacy's caves were carved out from a sandstone cliff overlooking the River Eden.

Lieutenant Colonel Samuel Lacy, who lived in Salkeld Hall in the 18th century, set his men to work on building these caves. Their exact purpose is unclear. They may have been made as wine cellars, or merely as "romantic" features of the landscape (a conceit much in vogue at that time) in which he could entertain friends. It is even said that Lacy employed a man to give the caves an authentic appearance by living in them as a hermit!

Retrace your steps to the main path. Climb up some steps to the cliff top, then descend the other side, almost to water level. Here is an avenue of trees, more evidence of Lacy's creative landscaping.

As you follow the path there are lots of rivulets flowing down the hillside to join the Eden. But you won't get your feet wet, because there are an equal number of tiny wooden bridges. Carry on through woodland, with a profusion of harebell and campion flowers in sea-

son, over a stile to arrive in open fields. Beyond a slight incline, bear slightly away from the river as the path levels out. Cross a stile and descend steps to a road.

Turn left along the road, but only for 100 yards. On the left is a path, way-marked "Eden Bridge". The path itself is not apparent, so just head back towards the river. Negotiate a stile and join a farm track that sticks to the riverside. When you are almost level with houses on the far side of the river, bear slightly away from the river to arrive at a pair of adjacent field-gates. After another gate you will arrive at Eden Bridge.

The walk continues from here to Kirkoswald, but if you want to take a look — or stay — at the village of Lazonby, cross Eden Bridge and follow the road.

Assuming you take the latter course, you'll be happy to know that almost the first building you will encounter in the

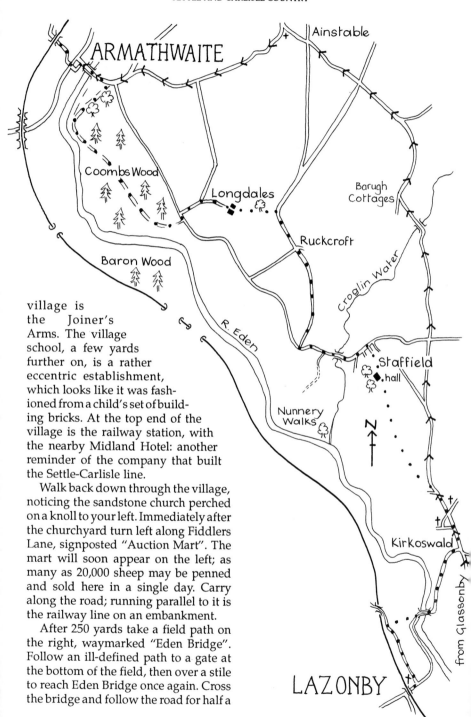

village is the Joiner's Arms. The village school, a few yards further on, is a rather eccentric establishment, which looks like it was fashioned from a child's set of building bricks. At the top end of the village is the railway station, with the nearby Midland Hotel: another reminder of the company that built the Settle-Carlisle line.

Walk back down through the village, noticing the sandstone church perched on a knoll to your left. Immediately after the churchyard turn left along Fiddlers Lane, signposted "Auction Mart". The mart will soon appear on the left; as many as 20,000 sheep may be penned and sold here in a single day. Carry along the road; running parallel to it is the railway line on an embankment.

After 250 yards take a field path on the right, waymarked "Eden Bridge". Follow an ill-defined path to a gate at the bottom of the field, then over a stile to reach Eden Bridge once again. Cross the bridge and follow the road for half a mile into Kirkoswald — a very attractive village, its little cobbled square surrounded by no fewer than three pubs.

Kirkoswald has more than once claimed the Cumbria Best Kept Village Award. There are many fine houses either side of the narrow main street. The church, built into the side of a hill topped by a detached bell tower, is reached by a delightful paved path. Notice the ancient wooden archway which forms part of the porch. Against the church wall is a well dedicated to Oswald, King of Northumbria from 634-642; now the origin of the village's name is quite clear.

Follow the road up the hill; where it forks, take the road ahead, signposted "Armathwaite". Just beyond the last house in the village take a field path on the left, waymarked "Staffield". Walk diagonally across the field to the far right corner. Go through a gate and walk along the field edge. At the brow of the hill you will see your next objective directly ahead: Staffield Hall, surrounded by trees.

Continue through a couple of kissing gates into open parkland. As you reach the grounds of the hall you will see a rather novel wrought-iron gate, which was designed to rotate around a central spindle in the manner of a revolving door. Don't enter the grounds, however, but take the kissing gate a few yards to the right. The iron field gate next to it is fitted with a rather unusual handle for opening and closing it.

Walk straight ahead, keeping the hall to your left, to join a road. Turn left along the road, go down a hill, and over a beck called Croglin Water. A hundred yards beyond the bridge you will find a pair of gates and a sign: "Nunnery House and Walks". Pay the 35p admission fee and take an hour or two out from the main walk to explore these delightful riverside walks. William Wordsworth, not a bad judge in these matters, reckoned that the Nunnery Walks in general —

and the waterfalls of Croglin Water in particular — comprised some of the finest vistas in the area.

The hall — built in 1715 — is on the site on an earlier Benedictine nunnery, and the walks themselves were laid out much later. Cross the lawn in front of the house and follow an obvious footpath. There is a map mounted a hundred yards from the house, as you begin the walks, which indicates a choice of three routes. Take the longest one, unless your feet are aching or time is pressing. It accompanies the river Eden for about a mile and a half, though it comes to a dead-end. There is, alas, no right of way to continue any further along the riverbank towards Armathwaite. So whether you choose a long or short stroll, you will eventually need to retrace your steps to the hall.

The first part of the walk follows Croglin Water as it cascades, somewhat unexpectedly, down a steep-sided ravine, in a succession of waterfalls. Then both beck and walker join the River Eden — glassily calm one moment, then rushing noisily over the rocks. Here the Eden flows through a rocky gorge; with its bluffs and pine trees, bracken and heather, the scene would not be out of place in the highlands of Scotland.

For a few yards, the riverside path is a ledge cut out of a sandstone cliff. The railway runs along the top of the gorge on the opposite side of the river, though you wouldn't be aware of it unless a train happened to be passing.

The woodland walks may be a riot of floral colour in the right season; at any time of the year the woods will be full of songbirds, tits and two little birds to be found creeping mouselike up the trunks of trees: treecreepers and nuthatches.

On arriving back at the hall, rejoin the road and follow it to the left. After a quarter of a mile take a road on the right, signposted "Ruckcroft and Ainstable"' The road climbs steadily, passing

Field barns are typical of the Eden Valley, though farming changes have made many obsolete.

through the small collection of houses that is Ruckcroft. If you look left — westwards — on a clear day, you will see some of the Lakeland peaks in the far distance, with the saddle-backed profile of Blencathra being the most prominent.

After the last farmhouse in the hamlet, take a foot-path on the left, waymarked

The Nunnery Walks offer a pleasant woodland ramble, with waterfalls, gorges and fine views of the River Eden.

"Longdales". Follow a path downhill, keep left of a small copse, and carry straight on to the farmstead ahead of you. On reaching the farm buildings, the path becomes a tarmac track, which rejoins the road.

Go left along the road for about 200 yards. On the right is a broad cinder track, waymarked "Armathwaite", which descends through a Forestry Commission conifer plantation, called Coombs Wood. Take this path through

The little sandstone church at Armathwaite is built neatly into the hillside.

the wood; notice how few birds you see and hear compared with the broad-leaved "native" woodlands on the Nunnery Walks.

The track you are walking was an old timber road made in the 18th century when this area was first planted by the Earl of Carlisle.

When the track forks, take the right-hand path. Soon you will find yourself in less oppressive woodland, among silver birch trees and gorse. The river Eden can be seen again to the left; beyond it are the nine arches of the Armathwaite viaduct.

Keep on this well-defined path until you arrive at the rear of the Fox and Pheasant Inn.

Turn left along the road, cross the river bridge and enter the trim little village of Armathwaite. Bear left around a bend, and then — if you want the railway station — take the first road on the right which climbs steeply up to the station.

● **CYCLE TRAIL:** Leave Langwathby on the road heading north, to the village of Little Salkeld. On the way to Glassonby, make a slight detour to investigate the fascinating stone circle known as Long Meg and Her Daughters. A smaller detour, soon after, will allow you to explore the 14th century Addingham church, sitting on its own about half a mile from Glassonby. It was built to replace an earlier church, standing on the river-bank, which was swept away by floods.

At Glassonby, the trail parts company with the Cumbria Cycle Way. At this point, instead of going right towards Renwick, bear left to the pleasant village of Kirkoswald. Take the road to Staffield, bearing right at a fork to head for Ainstable.

From there you have only about a mile, mostly downhill, until you cross the bridge over the River Eden and pedal on towards the hostelries of Armathwaite. ❏

Armathwaite to Carlisle

The final section of the walk — 14 miles (25 km) — accompanies the River Eden and winds through woodland up to the historic border city of Carlisle, with its ancient fortifications.

ARMATHWAITE has had numerous spellings. One of the earliest forms was "Ermitetwayth", and is thought to refer to a real hermit. Less of a supposition is the meaning of "thwaite", a common suffix in place names indicating "a clearing in the forest".

Armathwaite Castle, situated on the riverside, was originally a pele tower offering a line of defence against raiders from the north. It was the seat of the Skelton family, one of whose members, John Skelton, was Poet Laureate during the reigns of Henry VII and VIII. His poems were not, however, universally acclaimed, and he was forced to seek sanctuary in Westminster Abbey following the less than appreciative reception accorded to his satires on Cardinal Wolsey.

Leave Armathwaite, going north, on the road signposted to "Lockhills and Wetheral". Pass the tiny sandstone church, up on your left: it's the very epitome of unostentatious simplicity, and none the worse for that. The plain rectangular shape is uninterrupted even by a porch. The interior is dominated by three spans of wooden roof-beams. Close by is the old schoolhouse, with a little bell tower, inscribed plaque and a clock set into the outside wall.

You soon get good views down to the right into the Eden valley, while on the left the Settle-Carlisle railway runs parallel to the road, on an embankment.

Peaceful villages all along the line received an influx of "navigators" while the railway was being built, and Armathwaite was no exception. The good news was the extra trade the navvies brought: the publicans were certainly very happy and wages were never higher. The down side was a resultant increase in gambling, poaching and fighting.

One scrap between navvies ended fatally and the murderer — a man called Sampson — lay low by the river bank near Armathwaite Bridge, in a cave still known as Sampson's Cave. Nevertheless he was apprehended, taken to Carlisle and summarily hanged.

When the line crosses a small valley on a seven-arched viaduct, take a road to the right signposted "Low House". Follow the road as it bears left past a farm and becomes an unmade track. The route carries on down to the banks of the River Eden; you will be seeing a good deal of it over the next few miles.

Pass Low House, its grounds surrounded by high walls. At this point there is a long island in the river. Walk along a pleasant wooded track. Soon the track climbs uphill. To the right is your path — waymarked "Wetheral" — that wanders through woodland and follows the riverside. The scene hereabouts is somewhat reminiscent of the Nunnery Walks, especially as you pass some weather-worn sandstone cliffs.

This was once the site of Wetheral Priory; the priory has long since disappeared, leaving the gatehouse in splendid isolation.

Keep a look-out for Dippers and ducks — not just the ubiquitous Mallard but more exotic species too, such as Gooseanders and Goldeneyes.

Soon you walk through more level pasture; the cliffs are now to be found on the opposite bank of the river. Pass a wooden summer-house and a short stretch of sandy beach. On reaching a fence and more woodland, bear left up a steep hill; at the top turn right after a stile and follow the track marked "Wetheral".

Walk along the edge of a field, with a fence and woodland directly to your right. The path follows the contours of the wood, over stiles waymarked with yellow arrows. Watch out for a path to the right, waymarked as before, which takes you steeply down to the riverside once again.

Follow a delightful sandy path along the river. Notice a couple of huts — one green hut has a pair of matching din-

ghies moored close by. Walk through woodland, both coniferous and deciduous. Whenever you find the path indistinct, there will be little yellow arrows to guide you.

Opposite is another island in the river. Your path now takes you through open pasture for about a mile, then back into woodland. You will hear — if not see — any Settle-Carlisle train that happens to be passing: you are very close to the line at this point in the walk.

After more pasture there's another wood, as you notice a farm up to your left. The riverside path continues to alternate through fields and woods. The path itself is unobtrusive: with "improvements" only where really necessary, such as the odd footbridge or duckboard to keep your feet dry when the going gets soggy.

A third island coincides with the path leaving the river; a yellow arrow guides you into scrubland and bracken. The

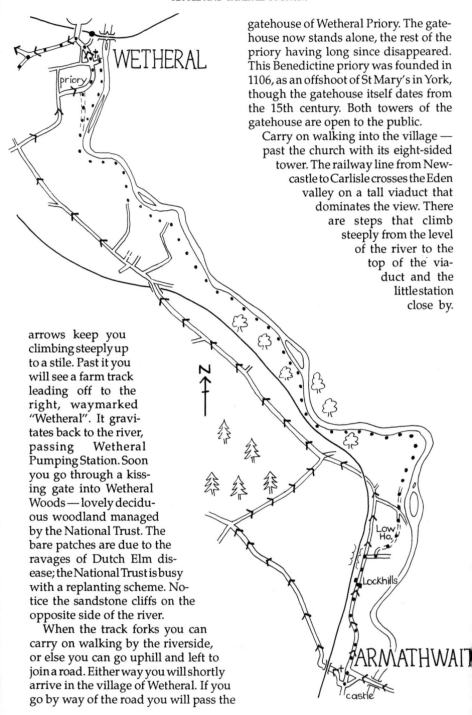

gatehouse of Wetheral Priory. The gate-house now stands alone, the rest of the priory having long since disappeared. This Benedictine priory was founded in 1106, as an offshoot of St Mary's in York, though the gatehouse itself dates from the 15th century. Both towers of the gatehouse are open to the public.

Carry on walking into the village — past the church with its eight-sided tower. The railway line from New-castle to Carlisle crosses the Eden valley on a tall viaduct that dominates the view. There are steps that climb steeply from the level of the river to the top of the viaduct and the little station close by.

arrows keep you climbing steeply up to a stile. Past it you will see a farm track leading off to the right, waymarked "Wetheral". It gravitates back to the river, passing Wetheral Pumping Station. Soon you go through a kissing gate into Wetheral Woods — lovely deciduous woodland managed by the National Trust. The bare patches are due to the ravages of Dutch Elm disease; the National Trust is busy with a replanting scheme. Notice the sandstone cliffs on the opposite side of the river.

When the track forks you can carry on walking by the riverside, or else you can go uphill and left to join a road. Either way you will shortly arrive in the village of Wetheral. If you go by way of the road you will pass the

If you want to cross the valley, and investigate the adjacent village of Great Crosby, you can stroll along the viaduct. A walkway keeps you well away from the trains, and you get a bird's-eye view of the river valley below.

One incentive to cross the viaduct might be the pub you can see on the Great Crosby side, though there are other watering holes in Wetheral itself, including the Crown Hotel, just a few yards from the station.

If your riverside rambles have left you exhausted, you can hop on a train here. Wetheral is the last stop on the line before Carlisle. Otherwise, pick up your feet and leave the village by the road marked "Scotby and Carlisle".

Immediately after a Methodist Chapel, take a road to the left, signposted "Wetheral Pasture". The road soon bears left; take a right-hand track here, waymarked "Scotby".

A bridge over a beck has been cunningly constructed from three large-gauge pipes laid side by side, allowing water to flow through and tractors to drive over. Follow the track; it skirts farm buildings and goes through a gate into a field. Follow the arrowed path, keeping a hedge to your left. Go through a kissing gate to follow a track to the right.

Go underneath the railway line and carry straight on, ignoring a footpath to your left, waymarked "Cumwhinton". After a few more yards, take a path on the right through a gate. You approach the Settle-Carlisle railway again, and cross it on a small bridge. Beyond the bridge, continue on the path to the left, till it comes out onto a road. Walk along the road and turn right at a T-junction, this brings you into the village of Scotby.

The road bears sharp left, and then sharp right, past a church on a knoll. Go

With Scottish raiders an ever-present threat, Carlisle Castle was under siege on a number of occasions.

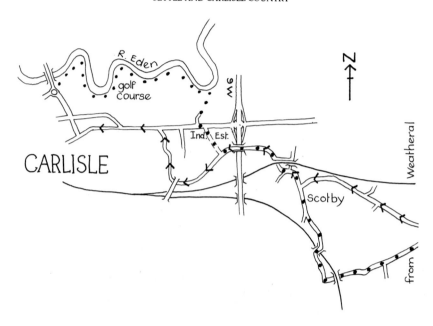

under a bridge and take the first road, immediately on the left. Follow this road until it crosses a bridge over the M6 motorway. Then turn first right, past a few houses and into an industrial estate. Beyond the car showrooms and wholesalers you meet a main road; cross it and take a track to the right.

Go to the right of a corrugated iron building, and pass a few picnic tables, until you reach, for the last time in this walk, the banks of the river Eden. Take a stile to your left and walk along the river, towards the city of Carlisle, whose taller buildings can be seen on the skyline.

This is level, easy walking through meadowland, with sheep for company. As you skirt a golf course, notice small holes in the sandy river bank opposite. These are the nesting holes of the Sand Martin, a little bird that comes here each summer and then seldom strays far from running water.

Having followed the river around large sweeping curves, you arrive in Carlisle: journey's end...

● **CYCLE TRAIL:** Leave Armathwaite going north, as for the walking route. For the next few miles you are never more than a few hundred yards from both the River Eden on your right and the Settle-Carlisle line, which you cross twice — first over, then under — before arriving in Wetheral. The village sits one side of a gorge, with the Eden running through and the village of Great Corby on the far side.

Take a road, west, to Scotby; from here then go over the M6 motorway and follow signs for Carlisle. For the last mile you join the A69 road as it enters Carlisle. ❏

Short excursions

Country footpaths are often very old indeed, and bridges may rely on unfamiliar technology. This fine example of a clapper bridge was spotted by the author, not far from Kirkby Stephen.

FOLLOWING the ten sections of the Settle & Carlisle Way, here are ten more walks to explore further some of the countryside in the environs of the railway. Most of these walks start and finish at one of the stations on the line, making them ideal for walkers who also want to use the train. After all, a train ride on this most scenic of lines can be a relaxing way to end a day's walk.

The walks are shorter than the sections of the Settle & Carlisle Way, making them ideal for half-day rambles, or for families with small children.

1. Saltaire circular

A leisurely stroll of about three miles around the model village built by Sir Titus Salt to house the workers at his gigantic textile mill nearby.

SALTAIRE is a model village built between 1850-60 by that great mill-owner and patriarch, Sir Titus Salt, to house the workers at his textile mill — at one time the largest in the world.

In time-honoured Victorian tradition he wanted to cater for his workers' spiritual as well as material needs. So Sir Titus built churches, institutes and schools, as well as a park in which his workers could relax at the weekend. But not too strenuously, since Sir Titus would personally banish from his park anyone whose behaviour was less than decorous!

Sobriety was another trait that Sir Titus encouraged in his workers. The one amenity missing from his model village was a public house, and Saltaire is "dry" to this day. Nevertheless, Sir Titus was not averse to having a bottle of fine port on his own table.

Sir Titus Salt's great mill spans the canal, forming a broad stone canyon; its chimney in the form of a Venetian Campanile is a notable attraction. As you walk up Victoria Street you will see the magnificent Congregational Church on the left (reckoned by many to be the finest non-conformist church in Britain), the town hall, school, former canteen, almshouses, and rows of solid, well-made homes. Note that all the streets are named after Victoria and Albert, Sir Titus himself, and then all the members of his family — in strict order of importance.

Go down to the bridge over the canal, and straight ahead to the footbridge spanning the River Aire. Before crossing it, you might call in at the little boathouse. It was built by Sir Titus in 1871, and is now converted into a Victorian theme restaurant.

Cross the river into Roberts Park, where a bronze statue was erected in 1903 to mark the centenary of his birth. Sir Titus died in 1876 and was buried in the specially built mausoleum attached to Saltaire Church.

Walk directly ahead through the park, emerging through the rear exit. Bear left along the way, signposted "Shipley Glen". Cross the road and follow the tarmac path between the school and the playing field, which will bring you to the tramway.

Shipley Glen tramway was built late last century by Sam Wilson, a local entrepreneur. It is a very unusual cable-hauled tramway leading to the top of the Glen; it was recently restored by the Bradford Trolleybus Association. Apart from saving a steep climb, it's worth the 15p for a lovely nostalgic ride in a brightly painted red car through overhanging woods. Significantly, the ride down costs just 10p! If the tramway is not in operation (it is open at weekends and main holiday times) a path runs parallel to the track.

At the top of the Glen are the remains of what was a quite extensive Victorian pleasure park, now a small funfair. Keep ahead along the suburban road to the Old Glen House Café (refreshments, toilets). You now find yourself on Baildon Green, an area of open common land covered with grass and gritstone boulders. Make your way along a choice of paths with the road to your left, the Glen to your right.

"Shipley Glen" is a Victorian misnomer; it is actually a typical Pennine gill which happens to be in Baildon. Nevertheless it has long been a popular area for strolling and sight-seeing.

Keep ahead for about 200 yards. On the right you will notice a farmhouse with what appears to be a white outhouse in front. This is Bracken Hall Countryside Centre. Call in (it's open most days) to enjoy a range of exhibitions featuring the geology, natural history and local history of Shipley Glen and Baildon Moor.

You will also see from the large-scale maps on display, the prehistoric stone circle on the green quite close to the

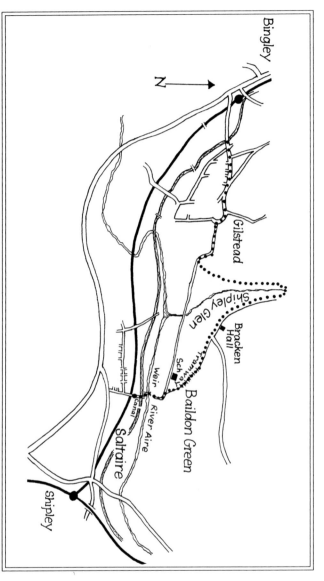

centre. The route continues along the green for another half mile, as it narrows between road and Glen. Almost at the end, a signposted path bears left down to the beck, going between two round concrete posts down to a stone bridge over the stream. Cross it, but almost immediately turn left off the main path to take a narrow way up the hillside for about ten yards. Then bear left again along a clear path which goes along the hillside down to the Glen.

This is a beautiful woodland path. Although you are close to the edge of the town and suburban housing, there is an impression of being deep in a typical Pennine woodland. It's not hard to see how this area must have looked before man's influence was felt: the oak, alder and birch trees growing out of the gritstone crags.

Keep on the path for a good half mile, until you reach the mouth of the Glen, with ponds below, the wood opening out into the main Airedale valley and the path curving right by trees before entering a narrow walled path. Go right; this leads to a gate into a broader lane.

Turn left almost immediately onto another signposted path. It runs initially along the edge of a field, and then between walls. It drops steeply through a wood to cross a stream before ascending steps. Curving round the outside of a high-walled garden, it bears left to join the road.

You are now in Gilstead, a suburb of Bingley. Turn right, uphill, to the road junction, then left into Gilstead Lane past St Wilfrid's Church. Keep ahead along the road for about 150 yards before forking left down Fernicliffe Road.

There are magnificent views from here across Airedale, part industrial, part rural, and typical of this part of the old West Riding. Bingley is spread out below, its surviving mill chimneys and weaving sheds contrasting with the massive modernistic bulk of the Bradford and Bingley Building Society. Beyond the town is a fine expanse of woodland and moorland, lending the scene a certain grandeur.

Follow the road downhill to where it crosses the canal. To the left is a gap leading down to the canal towpath. From here it is no more than five minutes walk to Bingley town centre; alternatively you can turn left for the two-mile walk along the main Settle-Carlisle Way back to Saltaire. ❑

Right: The splendid Congregational Church at Saltaire, built by industrialist and philanthropist, Sir Titus Salt.

2. Bingley St Ives

VISITING THE DRUID'S ALTAR

A four-mile (7km) ramble from industrial Bingley, which soon offers woodland walking, gritstone crags and extensive views over the Aire valley.

THIS short walk from Bingley explores a superb central section of Airedale. From Bingley railway station, cross to the main Bradford road, turning right to the traffic lights. Keep ahead to the next set of traffic lights by the parish church and the old White Horse pub, turning left along the Harden and Cullingworth Road. Cross the river by the Brown Cow pub and Harden Bridge.

Take the first turning on the right (you might just spot a narrow ginnel between houses; otherwise take the more obvious track). This swings right past houses and mill buildings, and leads to a delightful riverside area, part of Bingley Gorge, going past the backs of gardens and the playing fields of Bingley Grammar School.

The track you follow is a farm track, with the river on your right and the dense woodlands of Hollin Oak Plantation to the left. The track swings away from the river and soon reaches Raven Royd Farm, going round stables and farm buildings and on up the valley. The track eventually becomes a field path alongside the wall and woodland. Keep ahead through gates, the path bearing slightly left by a hillock before dipping towards Marley Farm. Bear left through small enclosures to emerge on a track above the farm. Go left again, climbing uphill past the entrance to Hutler Hill Farm, and up a shallow ravine filled with bracken and blackberries, the track soon sweeping up the hillside of Marley Brow.

Where the track turns sharp left again into fields, your way is through the stile ahead. Take a narrow, winding path through heather, bracken and scrub woodland. Keep straight on almost to the brow of the hill, before turning left along a clear path which follows the moor edge alongside a dry-stone wall. This is a beautiful path, offering magnificent views across the valley which, in spite of industry, suburban development and an unsightly new road, is still a true Yorkshire Dale, with typical green valley sides capped by open brown moorland.

Follow the path along the moorside which soon leads into an area of gritstone outcrops and bracken, and finally to a number of craggy rocks overlooking the valley, the largest of these being the superb viewpoint known as Druid's Altar. Benjamin Disraeli came to Bingley in the 1850s to visit his friends, the Ferrands of St Ives, and he later used these crags in his novel *Sybil*, as a setting for a meeting of Chartists.

From Druid's Altar bear right to the parallel track, and look for a stile in the park wall. This leads into St Ives Estate, a beautiful countryside park high above Airedale, which is owned by Bradford Corporation.

Turn right along the main path, across another stile and into an area of woodland. Walk into the estate, past the golf course. Keep on the main path as it swings to the left, entering an area of rampant rhododendron bushes. Soon, as the path begins to descend, another area of wind-carved gritstone is passed on the left. This is Lady Blantyre's rock, so called because it was a favourite rest-

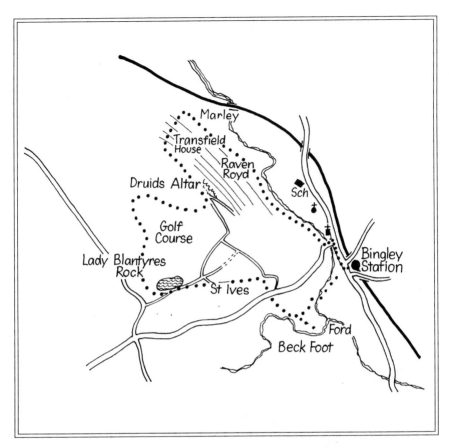

ing place of Lady Blantyre of the Ferrand family. There is a commemorative plaque which recalls her and, nearby, a memorial to the reforming zeal of her son-in-law, Edward Ferrand, the owner of the estate and a progressive Victorian Member of Parliament.

The path descends through trees to crossroads. Turn left, the way now going along the edge of a lake, Coppice Pond. The path emerges at the tarmac road leading to the house, St Ives, a Victorian mansion now used as a golf clubhouse. Refreshments are available from the conservatory during the summer months.

Cross towards the house. Unless you seek refreshment, however, take the path which runs below the lawns and on the edge of the parkland to join the main drive. Turn right, descending towards the main road, but about 100 yards before the entrance, as the drive curves to the right, look for a path on the left which cuts across the corner to the main Bingley-Cullingworth road.

This path branches left alongside the road for another 100 yards and emerges at a stile. Cross the road and locate a stile almost opposite. This leads to a lovely stepped path through dense oak woods which descends to an open grassy area by the riverside. Ahead is the metal footbridge which leads into Myrtle Park and the centre of Bingley.

It is worth taking time, however, to

Bingley is more than just a mill town — among interesting places to visit is this 16th century inn.

visit the beautiful little Beckfoot packhorse bridge, easily reached by taking a path that bears right at the bottom of the oak woods. It leads alongside the river on a narrow way to the little arched bridge, in its woodland setting, at the bottom of Beckfoot Lane. ❑

3. The Worth Valley

A six-mile (11km) walk up the valley which boasts not only a fine restored railway, but — of course — the literary mecca which was home to the Brontës.

This walk starts from Keighley, finishes in Oxenhope, and takes in the literary Mecca of Haworth. Using part of the Worth Way between Keighley and Oxenhope stations, it makes an ideal short day's walk from Keighley station on the Leeds-Settle-Carlisle line. For the return journey from Oxenhope to Keighley, you may wish to take one of the steam or diesel engines which ply the Worth Valley Railway line, which is claimed, with some justice, to be Britain's finest standard gauge private railway.

This, and other walks in the Worth Valley, are featured in *Worth Valley Rail Trail* by Hilary Darby. This book is published by the Worth Valley Railway Society and is available from the bookshops at both Keighley and Haworth stations.

You will find, as you walk, that much of the route is waymarked by the "Worth Way" railway engine motif, as well as by yellow arrows or blobs.

From the forecourt of Keighley station turn left towards the town centre, but go first left again down Low Mill Lane. Where the road bends left under the railway bridge, take the footpath (or "ginnel") that runs between high walls to the left through a tunnel. Eventually you reach a broad footbridge over the trackbed of the disused Great Northern Railway that once ran to Queensbury and Halifax. The path goes through another short stretch of tunnel to the main road. Note the three heads, one with a top hat, carved on the mill chimney to your right.

Cross the road to the left, but almost immediately go down a cul-de-sac lane — The Walk — towards some mill gates; just before these gates go left along another enclosed path. Follow this as it runs by the mill building, and then very attractively alongside the River Worth for about half a mile, finally reaching Woodhouse Road.

Turn left here, keeping ahead at the crossroads at Hainworth Wood Road, along the continuation of Woodhouse Road and past the Belhaven Pub. Carry on to where the road ends, past tall houses to locate another enclosed, cobbled path on the left which climbs steeply uphill. At the top there are superb views of Keighley and the suburbs which extend up the hillsides, with rural Airedale and Rombalds Moor beyond.

Take the stile on the left onto an unsurfaced road, keeping right for about 100 yards before another waymarked stile on the right leads into a little beech and sycamore copse. Keep ahead to an iron pedestrian gate in the wall corner, and cross the next field to a gate. Pick up a line of stiles alongside the wall on the right as the path follows the wall past Gingerbread Clough. As you approach Hainworth you go through a gap to keep the wall on the left, and you join a track past a farm into the village.

Hainworth is an unspoiled hilltop village, with several 18th century cottages, one of which has a fascinating motto and the date (1783) carved over the door. Walk through the centre of the village. The lane becomes a track which narrows to a beautiful path contouring

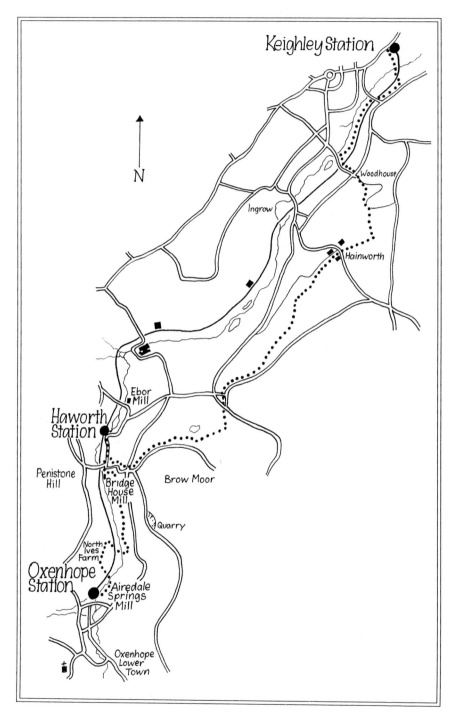

Pride of the Worth Valley — The City of Wells.

around the hillside. From here you can enjoy panoramic views across the Worth Valley towards Haworth and Penistone Hill on the right.

This path, broadening once again to a track, eventually joins the lane just above Barcroft. Turn right downhill through the village, keeping to the busy cross-roads (a one-way system) past the tall building known for some mysterious reason as Saltaire.

Cross the main Halifax-Keighley road with extreme care (traffic comes around

the corner at high speed). Take the track and bridleway opposite which bears off left, dipping down to swing left and climb back up to a group of cottages ahead on the hillside by the dripping factory. There can be a strong smell of bacon if you are down-wind of it.

Opposite the cottages a stile leads to a field path (not waymarked) which follows the edge of the field towards a small reservoir ahead. Before reaching the reservoir with its skirting of trees, the path bears left uphill through the heather to emerge alongside a wall and by the Three Sisters Country Hotel on Haworth Brow and Brow Moor.

Turn left, perhaps walking along the edge of the common, down to the crossroads with Hebden Road. Keep ahead down Brow Road as it hairpins steeply down to Bridge End and Station Road. Haworth Station is 200 yards to the right, and this makes a convenient end to the walk if time is short. You will find refreshments, a bookshop, an engine shed, and steam trains that will whisk you back to Keighley.

A path over the footbridge leads alongside the park and across the bypass to the centre of Haworth — a village that's known the world over as a literary shrine. It was in Haworth parsonage that the three Brontë sisters — Charlotte, Emily and Anne — grew up and honed the precocious writing skills that would later produce such famous novels as *Wuthering Heights* and *The Tenant of Wildfell Hall*. Brother Branwell misused his own literary talents, preferring to frequent Howarth's less salubrious ale-houses, and came to what is generally regarded as "a bad end".

Their mother and two other sisters died within five years of their arrival in Haworth. Anne and Emily died before they could enjoy any of the acclaim that was to greet their novels. Only Charlotte survived long enough to marry, though tragically she too died within a year of her wedding. The reverend Brontë survived all his daughters, and lived to the age of 84.

Almost a million visitors a year make the literary pilgrimage to Haworth. They can see the Brontë museum in the old parsonage and imagine what Haworth must have been like when the Brontë sisters were alive. It's a miracle that any "atmosphere" survives at all, because the cobbled main street has been transformed into another kind of shrine: dedicated to the commercial exploitation of the Brontë name.

Brontë buffs can stride across the windswept moors, just as the three sisters were wont to do, and visit Top Withens, the ruined farmhouse that is supposed to have been the model for *Wuthering Heights*. The Brontë Way is a circular walk, well waymarked, which takes in a number of other sites that claim connections, however tenuous, with Charlotte, Emily and Anne.

To complete the walk to Oxenhope, return to the Bridge End at the end of Station Road, continuing past the war memorial and the handsome Butterfield Mill. When Brow Road begins to climb uphill, turn right along a narrow, stepped path signed "Upper Gate, Oxenhope". This becomes a field path, partially flagged, which joins the side of a millrace, and follows Bridgehouse Beck and the course of the mill-race down the valley before crossing the mill-race at a footbridge.

Keep straight ahead along the waymarked path which curves round to join a beautiful, single-span packhorse bridge over Bridgehouse Beck, known locally as "Donkey Bridge".

You do not cross the bridge; continue instead down the valley. The path curves away from the stream for a short distance before joining the bridlepath that comes under the railway from North Ives. North Ives, on the hillside to the right, is a beautiful 17th century farmhouse. It was used extensively as a setting during the filming of *The Railway Children* and is also accessible by footpath.

Ignoring an enclosed path to the left, cross the stream again. Your path winds past the sewage works, recrosses the stream and becomes another attractive enclosed way which emerges at Oxenhope Station Road about 100 yards east of the station.

The station and its extensive yard have been beautifully refurbished with

The parsonage at Haworth where the Brontë sisters honed their precocious literary skills.

considerable attention to period detail. There is an excellent cafeteria in a stationary carriage where tea, coffee and hot snacks are available at the end of your walk.

The preservation of old trains and lines may be familiar today, but in 1962, when the Worth Valley line was resurrected, it was a rather novel idea. Nevertheless, a team of volunteer workers have managed to maintain a regular year-round timetable of steam trains running along five miles of track down the Worth Valley.

The line has recently been voted Britain's Independent Railway of the Year. The steam trains and stations have also been featured in films and TV productions, such as *The Railway Children, A Woman of Substance* and *The Adventures of Sherlock Holmes.* Devotees of steam locomotives will not be disappointed.

A rail ticket for your return journey to Keighley will also give you access to the Oxenhope Railway Museum, which is housed in the large engine shed opposite the station. It is here that many of the Worth Valley Railway's historic and larger engines are stored, including the L&Y 0-6-0 which featured so prominently in *The Railway Children,* together with historic carriages and a variety of station and signal-box signs from many long-vanished railway systems.

Fortunately, neither the Keighley-Oxenhope branch nor the Settle-Carlisle line — both at one time under threat of oblivion — have shared such a melancholy fate, and remain to delight future generations. ❏

4. Victoria Cave

A CIRCULAR WALK FROM SETTLE

A four-mile (7km) ramble through spectacular limestone scenery, taking in the cave where one man and someone else's dog made a major archaeological discovery.

THIS short walk in Upper Ribblesdale is ideal for a family ramble, being rich in history and offering spectacular views.

Take the steep lane from the northeast corner of Settle market place, which climbs past cottages; this is Constitution Hill. Where the lane forks, immediately above the town, keep right uphill along an enclosed way, going through a gate. This soon becomes a stony track. At the next gate, keep straight ahead alongside the wall, through two more gates.

This path is an ancient packhorse way, almost certainly first developed by the monks of Fountains Abbey as part of a network of routes through Ribblesdale, linking outlying granges and crossing over to Malhamdale.

There are soon fine views up Ribblesdale and towards the Three Peaks, across to and beyond the village of Langcliffe. Where the path enters an open field, bear slightly right towards a wood ahead. Go through a gate below the

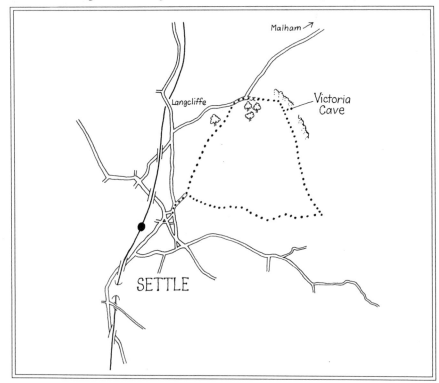

Victoria Cave lies on a major fault in the Craven Dales limestone which has created the impressive Giggleswick Scar, Malham Cove and Goredale Scar. A parallel fault line has produced a secondary ridge, as shown here at Crummackdale.

wood. Follow the wall and go through another gate. Keep ahead to join the Langcliffe-Malham road.

Turn right here, but as the lane swings left, keep ahead through a gate. Follow the track alongside the wood which bears left and climbs steeply upwards towards the line of rocky scars ahead.

Immediately below the crags — Langliffe Scar — turn right through a gate and over an iron stile to follow the path alongside the wall. After about 400 yards, almost opposite the line of a ruined wall, look for a path which winds up the scree to Victoria Cave. You will find a natural cavern in the rock face which affords spectacular views across Rib-

blesdale and over to the Forest of Bowland, whose line of hills forms the horizon ahead.

Victoria Cave is one of the most fascinating archaeological sites in Britain. It was discovered by accident in 1838 when a local man, Michael Horner, was walking a friend's dog. The dog vanished into the hillside and reappeared several yards away. Puzzled, Horner soon rounded up a group of friends — including local archaeologist Joseph Jackson—to help excavate the immense cave.

It proved to be an archaeological treasure house. In the floor of the cave were remains of animals such as the bison, rhinocerous, elephant, bear and hyena. There were relics, too, of Stone Age Man, dating from around 10,000BC, as well as of later peoples from Iron Age and Romano-British times, who left jewellery, pottery and tools. It appears likely that the cave was used as a hiding place during the Roman occupation; many were the skirmishes with the Picts and Scots during those troubled times.

A lot of these discoveries found their way into the British Museum, in London, though some can be seen in the Museum of North Craven Life in Settle. The cave was named in honour of the young Queen Victoria, who was crowned the year the cave was discovered.

Return on the linking path to the main footpath, continuing left along the path. At a stone stile, the path bears right to a wall below. Continue to the wall corner and follow the path ahead. At a gate turn right.

You are now in an area of spectacular limestone scenery. There are crags, scars and weathered pinnacles: a kind of miniature Dolomites, rich in caves. To the left is Attermire Scar, to the right Warrendale Knots.

Follow the wall downhill. Go over a stile and follow the wall to a gap ahead. Then bear right, slightly uphill, along a faint path to the wall and keep ahead to the wall corner.

Go through the gate here and down a beautiful green track, now enjoying spectacular views over the rooftops of Settle. You soon rejoin the track taken on the outward journey. Turn left through the gate back onto the enclosed track down to Constitution Hill and back into Settle. ❏

5. Crummackdale

A six-mile (14km) tour of the grikes and clints of limestone country, via walled green lanes, and a look at a controversial local industry.

HORTON-IN-RIBBLESDALE is the sort of place that people tend to drive through without stopping. And it's true that Horton's main claim to fame is its position, smack in the middle of the famous Three Peaks: Ingleborough, Whernside and — closest of all — Pen y Ghent.

This walk takes in some fascinating limestone scenery, follows delightful enclosed paths and accompanies the River Ribble. There is also an insight into a controversial local industry.

Begin the walk at Horton railway station, reached from the village by walking northwards along the main road. You are walking away from the distinctive profile of Pen y Ghent, though it remains a prominent landmark for much of the walk. Where the road bears sharp right, signposted to Hawes and Ribblehead, walk straight ahead, up to the station. Left of the station buildings is a footpath sign - to Crummackdale - which directs you over the railway line (watch out for trains) and up some steps on the other side.

Go through a gate into open fields. Keep straight ahead through a gap stile. Bear slightly right, to follow a distinct path. A farm is to the left and, beyond it, an extensive limestone quarry. Cross a farm track to a ladder stile. The path continues through rolling grassland, and bears slightly uphill to another ladder stile.

Here the landscape changes. The ground becomes stony underfoot, and limestone outcrops appear. You could almost be on another planet. Keep walk-ing uphill, through areas of limestone pavement. The limestone scenery of scars, pavements and caves is typical of the southern part of the Yorkshire Dales.

The strange, fissued appearance of the pavements was created during the last Ice Age, 15,000 years ago. Glaciers left the limestone exposed to the elements, then the rain gradually carved the soluble rock into the strange shapes we can see today. The rock shapes are known as clints, while the fissures between them are grikes. What may, at first, appear to be lifeless rock formations actually support a great variety of plantlife.

The Hawthorn is one of the few trees to thrive in this bleak habitat, and typically stunted examples, buffeted and bent by the prevailing wind, can be seen on this walk. Lichens cover the rounded clints, which both protect and nourish the larger plants that thrive in the grikes — such as the wavy leaves of the hart's-tongue fern.

At a small pile of stones the path forks. Take the left path, none too distinct, that soon follows the line of a wall. Take a ladder stile, waymarked "Aust-wick". Pick your way in and out of the limestone outcrops, then cross another ladder style over the wall. Pass grouse-shooting butts made, inevitably, from limestone.

Suddenly you find yourself standing at the edge of a natural amphitheatre, surrounded by limestone scars. Stop for a moment to admire the view down into a green valley which is very different

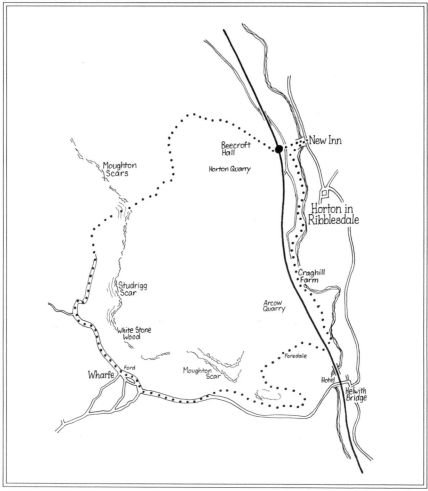

from the limestone terrain you have just been walking through. This is Crummackdale, a secret valley unseen by motorists.

A path leads down into the valley. Through a gate, take a delightful grassy path between walls. Enjoy easy walking through this undulating landscape of fields, walls and barns. Go through a couple of gates, and past sheep pounds, until you reach a T-junction of enclosed tracks. Turn right, for just a few yards, to where Austwick Beck is spanned by a splendid stone clapper bridge. Next to it

is a ford, and, just downstream, another footbridge. This one is constructed from a single slab of stone. If you want a peaceful spot to sit down and eat your sandwiches, then look no further.

Walk back to the T-junction of walled tracks, and carry straight on, downhill, as the path narrows. Pass a couple of field barns to arrive in the hamlet of Wharfe — a secluded huddle of houses

Right: A superb limestone pavement — the raised parts are known as clints, and the hollow troughs, grykes.

Crummackdale: a paradise for walkers, as the pictures on this and the facing page show so well.

and farms hidden even from the road between Austwick and Helwith Bridge. Keep left past the houses, to join the road. Bear left along it for 500 yards, then take a stepped stile on the left, waymarked "Horton-in-R".

Join an uphill gradient over two more stiles. As you climb over the third, there's a surprise waiting for you. Below you is the huge man-made canyon of Dry Rigg Quarry, one of the largest of the many quarries in the Horton area.

Depending on your viewpoint, you may see it as a valuable source of local employment, or merely a hideous eyesore. Less open to doubt is the way the quarry dominates the landscape; it has even bitten a large chunk out of Moughton Nab, a limestone scar that overlooks the workings. From a height

the lorries, diggers and bulldozers look like childs' toys as they trundle along the tracks that criss-cross the quarry.

Turn right at the quarry's edge, on a path waymarked "Foredale". Take a ladder style and join a cinder track which takes you in a wide arc, to skirt the perimeter of the quarry. When you reach the base of Moughton Nab, take a gate to the right. A path takes you down into Foredale, a cluster of houses which would not be out of place in Lakeland, being built of undressd slate instead of the usual stone construction typical of the Dales.

Carry on to join a tarmac track. This is the road used by laden lorries as they leave the quarry. After a few yards, go underneath the Settle-Carlisle railway. You will see signs here that indicate you

Sadly for the Dales, limestone is also a much sought-after commodity in a variety of industries and as hardcore for building roads. This eyesore is at Horton-in-Ribblesdale.

are joining the route of the Ribble Way, a long-distance footpath that explores the Ribble valley.

Soon you meet the River Ribble; ignore a footbridge and continue on what is now a stony track, as the river swings away to the right. Take a ladder stile into open fields, and along a slightly sunken way. When you meet up with the river again, bear left along the bank. Pass Cragghill Farm; don't take a footbridge over the river, but admire its construction out of a single huge length of wood.

You have pleasant easy walking through a copse, and over little footbridges across side-becks. Your way is clear: hugging the riverside. Many species of birds can be found along the river, such as Wagtails: yellow in summer, pied all the year round. Lapwings can be found in the fields nearby and other wading birds — such as Redshanks, Oystercatchers and Sandpipers — may be seen along the stony water margins of the river.

You soon arrive back in Horton, via stone steps which bring you to the river bridge and the Crown Inn. ❑

5. Dent Town

A walk of nine miles (16km) from the country's highest main line station to the delights of Dent, and then via the ancient packhorse route across the shoulder of Whernside.

THIS walk explores the top end of Dentdale, one of the most beautiful of the Dales, using part of the Dales Way footpath between Dent station and Dent. This is a fine walk at any time, but particularly in Spring when primroses fill the deep Dentdale hedgerows, themselves white with blackthorn or May blossom.

As with the Settle-Carlisle Way stages, this walk begins and ends at stations on the line. For the sake of variety, however, it is described from north to south. This walk can be used as a substitute for the section of the Way from Ribblehead to Garsdale, by following the instructions back-to-front. In case of difficulty with the route, OS 1:50,000 sheet 98 is recommended.

The beautiful village of Dent, with its whitewashed houses and cobbled streets, is well worth investigating. It makes an excellent place to stop for a leisurely lunch, before continuing the walk. This second half is a more strenuous hike, following the Craven Way, around Whernside — one of the famous Three Peaks — and on to Ribblehead.

Dent station makes a fine place from which to start a walk. At 1,150 feet above sea level it is the highest main line station in Britain.

Follow the steep road down from the station; there are extensive views of Dentdale at every turn, including Dent Head and Artengill viaducts. At Lea Yeat — once a Quaker Meeting House, but now a private dwelling — cross the bridge over the River Dee. Go through a gap stile in the far side of the bridge, which leads to the right along a lovely riverside path.

In dry weather this section of river vanishes into secret caverns, leaving the stony bed of the river often with little more than a trickle, but returning to spate after heavy rain. The path edges by a caravan site and copse to emerge in the lane at Ewegales Bridge.

Some 250 yards along the lane, look for a field gate facing you on the left. Go through it, following the track up towards the farm. Leave the track well before the farm buildings, to head straight on to a stile — part wood, part stone — immediately beyond a tiny stream. Cross it, keeping ahead through stiles through a dense conifer plantation below Little Town.

This path eventually emerges at a stile in the wall corner, left, at the end of the wood. Follow this wall to the next step stile beyond a barn to cross a track. Where this bends, keep ahead to a tall ladder stile by a tree. Cross to the next field to a stile leading into the drive of Coat Faw, a handsome Victorian house. Cross two ladder stiles, before following the wall right to Clint, keeping to the path below the house and garden to West Clint. Again, keep to the wallside, through a stile and over a bridge to High Lathe. Turn right to the gate in the road.

Go left along the lane for 200 yards, then take a field gate on the right. Carry straight across a field to a tiny and half-hidden bridge. Cross it and carry on ahead to Nelly Bridge over the River

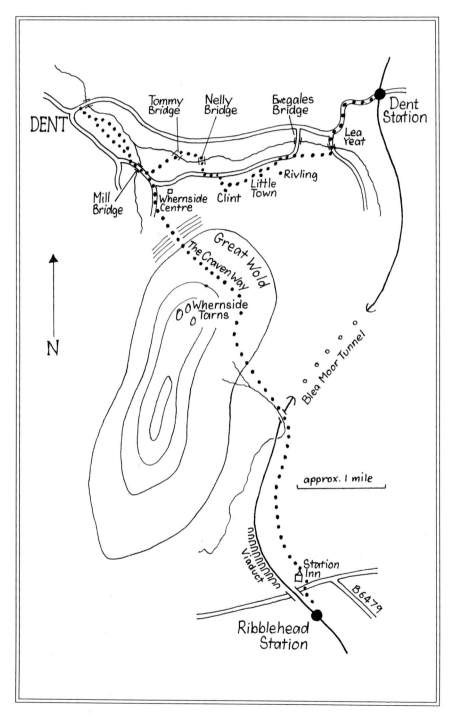

Dee. Follow the riverside for about half a mile, over stiles, to Tommy Bridge. Cross back over. Turn right through the gate, but bear left at the next gateway through a stile. Keep straight ahead to climb over the low hillock by a clump of trees before descending to Mill Bridge, where the abandoned sluice bed and millstones are evidence of the old cornmill.

Follow the path immediately to the right of Mill Bridge. This follows the Dee, over stiles, then along the flood embankment, turning right along Keld Beck to Church Bridge. Turn left along the road and walk into Dent Town.

Dent is a superb village. The only community larger than a hamlet in this extended valley, it reflects the scattered settlement patterns of the original Viking arrivals more than 1,000 years ago. Dent's ancient church, old grammar school and narrow cobbled streets reflect its former importance in a community whose main source of wealth was agriculture and hand-knitting — the so-called "terrible" (that is, "very fast") knitters of Dent.

There is a memorial fountain, fashioned from Shap granite, in the centre of the town's main street. It commemorates the life and work of Professor Adam Sedgwick, who was for fifty-five years the Professor of Geology at Cambridge University. He was one of the greatest scientific personalities of his day, an inspired teacher and a lifelong benefactor of his native dale.

The village has shops, cafés, a couple of excellent pubs and a tranquil air that hardly seems to belong to the twentieth century. Dent just squeezes inside the western boundary of the Yorkshire Dales, though it is actually in the county of Cumbria. Certainly, this delightful collection of white-washed cottages, huddled around the churchyard, seems to belong in spirit more to the Lake District than to the Dales.

Return to Mill Bridge by the same route you took earlier. (You can vary it slightly by taking the path which continues directly along Keld Beck to Double Croft farm). Carry on to the fork at the Methodist chapel by Whernside Manor, the former National Caving Centre which is now being developed as the Yorkshire Dales National Park's residential and study centre. Call in or pick up a leaflet at any National Park Centre for details of a wide range of educational and study courses in this lovely, reputedly haunted, setting. The hall's 18th century slave-owning occupants are also claimed by a local historian to have inspired Emily and Charlotte Brontë.

Bear right here along Dyke Hill Lane, but take the first track left. It soon becomes a stony track leading up the shoulder of Whernside Fell.

This is a steep but steady ascent, soon climbing several hundred feet; however your efforts will be rewarded by increasingly fine views across the valley. The track eventually levels to become a lovely green road. This is the Craven Way, once part of an ancient packhorse route linking Settle and Dent, but now a superb elevated route for walkers.

Where the track ceases to be enclosed, you can follow the wall, to the right, up to Whernside Tarns and the immense ridge that forms the summit of Whernside, returning to Ribblehead via Bruntscar. Another three miles (and at least an additional hour's walking) is required for this route — only recommended for strong walkers and in good visibility. Those who choose this high road will also be adding to the problem of intense erosion on the Three Peaks route. You have been warned...

Otherwise, follow the Craven Way as it gradually swings right, southwards, over the open moorland of Great Wold, following a line of limestone outcrops and shake holes. Soon you descend a

Top left *and* ***above:*** *Dent's main street — with its cobbles and whitewashed houses — is more reminiscent of the Lake District than the Dales. The fountain,with its piece of Shap granite, commemorates the village's most famous son, the geologist Adam Sedgwick.*
Left: *A stroll up Flintergill, to the south of Dent, is well worth the trouble.*

129

broad ridge. Note the line of brick turrets across the fell to your left —c these are the ventilation shafts of the 2,629-yard Blea Moor tunnel.

The track now becomes fainter in boggy ground. Go through the gate in the wire fence to meet other paths by Force Gill, and cross into Little Dale by an aqueduct over the Settle-Carlisle line. The path, muddy in places, follows the railway line by the lonely Blea Moor signal box. Keep ahead by Batty Moss; its grassy earthworks and tramway routes are the only remnants of the huge shanty town that once housed the navvies who built the viaducts and tunnels.

You will soon reach the monumental viaduct at Ribblehead, and, close by, the Station Inn for refreshment, or the station itself to await a southbound train.

❏

Right, top: Our walk to Dent begins at the country's highest main line station. The station buildings, on the left, are privately owned and were undergoing renovation at the time of publication. Note the remains of the snow fences on the right. The train is a diverted Glasgow to Paddington service. **Bottom:** *The view at Blea Moor on descending the old Craven Way packhorse route.*

7. Upper Wensleydale

*A linear walk of six miles (11km) which roughly
follows the line of the old Wensleydale Railway
to the busy market town of Hawes from where a
minibus service will return you to the station.*

FOR the walk to Hawes (a possible extension of Stage Five of the Settle-Carlisle Way), turn right outside Garsdale station and walk down the road past the phone box to the junction with the A684. Turn right along the road past Low Moor Farm, and under Dandry Mire Viaduct to the Moorcock Inn. Turn left for a short distance along the Kirkby Stephen road, to locate a farm track on the right, leading to Yore House farm.

The path crosses a bridge over the infant River Ure then swings round the back of the farm. Turn right along the wallside into rough pasture before bearing across with the contours to cross a shallow ravine, the line of the path marked by stiles and gates. Make for the narrow line of Cotterside plantation ahead, then cross another shallow ravine and beck, before bearing towards the riverside and Holmsett Plantation ahead. Carry straight on past another area of woodland to Thwaite Bridge. You reach the A684 at Thwaite Bridge House Farm.

Cross the road, almost immediately taking the path to Mossdale Head opposite, which climbs steeply along the edge of a recently planted hillside. A stile on the left leads across the river to Mossdale Farm, the viaduct carrying the trackbed of the old Hawes railway directly ahead.

Keep left along the field path which goes parallel to the river, marked by stiles. This follows a field wall and crosses pasture, but keeps to the right of a low hillock below Hill Wood End and Birkrigg Farm. The path is fairly easy to follow as it bears close to an attractive stretch of wooded riverside to emerge on the main road near Appersett by a ladder stile. However the path continues along the inside of the wall to a point near the Widdale Beck.

To avoid taking the main road into Hawes, turn right for 300 yards up the lane towards the old Appersett viaduct carrying the railway over the lane. A path starts immediately to the left of the viaduct and crosses due southeastwards — half left — across the field to a gate opposite. Keep ahead across a large open field before going left along the wallside ahead to a pretty area of woodland and waterfalls at Thorns. Follow the path to the left into Hawes town centre.

The characterful town of Hawes is known as the capital of Wensleydale, and for good reason. It's a bustling market town (markets every Tuesday), with an auction mart and a good array of shops. With its youth hostel, busy pubs and plentiful bed and breakfast accommodation, Hawes is a popular place for visitors.

It was in Hawes that the well-known Dalesman Kit Calvert resuscitated what was an ailing Wensleydale cheese industry, so that this local delicacy is once again widely available. Another local industry that caters for visitors is Outhwaite's, the rope-makers. Visitors can watch ropes being manufactured on the premises, and buy souvenirs from the gift shop.

The Wenseydale railway used to connect many of the villages in this broad dale, but it was closed down. The old

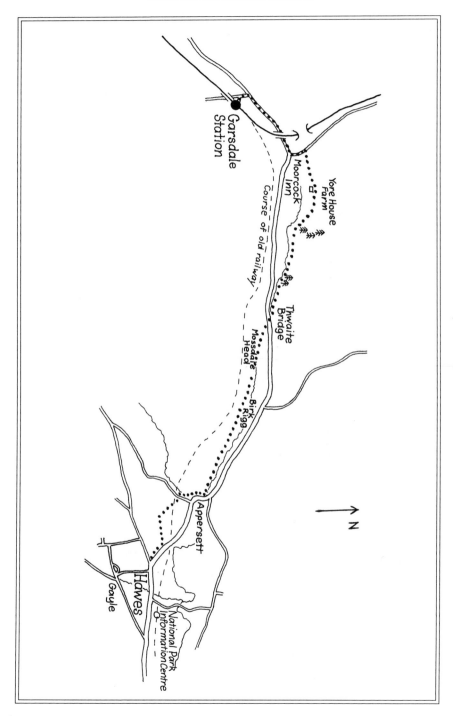

Gayle Beck, which runs through Hawes on its way to the River Ure, varies from a mere trickle in summer to a raging torrent after heavy rain.

Hawes station has been converted into a National Park information centre. (It is from here that the minibus leaves for the trip to Garsdale station). In an adjacent railway building is the Dales Countryside Museum, which houses a miscellany of bygones and curios — mostly donated by Dales historians Marie Hartley and Joan Ingilby — which help to bring the past to life.

Pennine Way walkers pass through both Hawes and the nearby village of Hardraw — site of England's highest single-drop waterfall. Hardraw Force falls ninety spectacular feet, from the top of a vertiginous crag into a shallow pool. The waterfall has been a popular attraction for many years; in its grand setting it conformed perfectly to the Victorian notion of the romantic landscape. More prosaically, visitors must now approach Hardraw Force via the bar of the Green Dragon pub, and a small charge is made.

Due to the excellent acoustics, brass band contests were regularly held in a bandstand near the waterfall, and the tradition was recently revived. But just to prove that things don't always go according to plan, the honours on one of the first occasions went to a band from Lancashire! ❑

Right: Hawes Parish Church, from the Pennine Way

8. Appleby Town Trail

An undemanding stroll around this attractive town which retains its medieval layout and hilltop castle.

APPLEBY was, until the boundary changes in 1974, the county town of Westmorland. It has since lost the title — and a lot of traffic too, now that the town is by-passed — but it has lost none of its charm. If possible, try to give yourself an hour or two to investigate its many attractions.

And yet it is for one particular event that Appleby is best known to the public at large. During the second week of June the town abandons its air of tranquil gentility for a week-long knees-up known as the Appleby Horse Fair, when horse traders, travelling people and a host of other visitors descend upon the town from all over the UK.

The horse fair is reputed to be the largest of its kind in the world. It is also said to have come into existence under a charter from King James II, in 1685, for the "purchase and sale of all manner of goods, cattle, horses, mares and geldings".

People come from far and wide to attend the fair, and camp out on Fair Hill. Traditional gypsy caravans can be seen parked side-by-side with modern mobile homes. Traders set up their stalls; fortune-tellers consult their crystal balls; children sell lucky charms.

When horses are being sold, they are staked out on the roadside for several miles around Fair Hill. They are put through their paces — to tempt potential buyers — in the lanes nearby. Traders take their horses for a wash in the river Eden, by the town bridge.

If you want to attend the fair, make sure you have your accommodation booked well in advance. There is no point in trying to find a bed for the night if you arrive during fair week without reservations. To add to the confusion, some pubs and inns close during fair week, while others are overflowing. Conversely, if you don't want to attend the fair, you know which week to avoid Appleby! The best fair days to come are Tuesday and Wednesday (the main sale day is Wednesday).

The town was incorporated as a borough by Henry II in 1174. Despite being burned and almost totally destroyed by Scottish raiders in 1388, the town retains its essentially medieval layout, with the exceptionally broad main street of Boroughgate running from the Norman castle down to the parish church.

Start the walk from Low Cross, at the bottom of Boroughgate, which marks the lower boundary of the market place. Set into the ground close by is a bull ring. It was last used in 1812, at a time when bull-baiting had already been made illegal. On that occasion a bull freed itself from its tethering and ran amok around the town, causing panic and injuries.

The Moot Hall sits a few yards away, on its island site. Above the door are the initials RAW and a date, 1596, though the hall was largely rebuilt after a fire. A plaque below the steps commemorates the town's charter of 1179. Assizes were held here until the late 18th century; the building now houses the Tourist Information Centre, while the town council sits upstairs.

Most of Boroughgate's buildings date

136

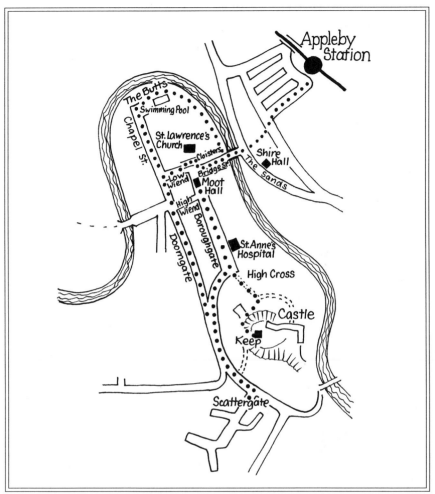

from the late 17th and early 18th centuries, and replaced Norman buildings that occupied the same sites. One of the earliest is a chemist's shop that still retains its 17th century frontage. The area just above the moot hall used to be the Shambles, a ramshackle collection of buildings that housed butchers and slaughtermen. The stench and filth from the Shambles led to their demolition in the 1880s, during a Victorian purge of unhygienic practices which also provided the town with a new water and sewerage system.

As you walk up Boroughgate, notice the White House, a Georgian Gothic extravagance built in 1756 for Jack Robinson, a local member of parliament. Have you ever wondered where the expression "before you can say Jack Robinson" came from? Well now you know...

A handsome avenue of lime trees stretches all the way up Boroughgate to the castle. They were planted in 1874 by bell-ringers from St Lawrence's Church.

One of Appleby's most delightful buildings is to be found on your left, as you walk up the hill. The Hospital of St Anne was built by Lady Anne Clifford and opened in 1653; it comprises tiny almshouses and a chapel for the use of "thirteen poor widows of the Estate". The doors to the almshouses open onto a tranquil little courtyard, complete with a fountain. The chapel contains a portrait of Lady Anne, and services are held here every Wednesday.

The High Cross at the top of Boroughgate marked the southern extent of the market. It bears the inscription: "Retain your loyalty, preserve your rights", and may have been erected by Jack Robinson on the base of an earlier cross. A cheese market was held here until the early years of this century.

Of all her six castles, Lady Anne Clifford regarded Appleby as her favourite. It is a fine example of motte and bailey construction, built before 1100, though within a century a Norman keep, later known as Caesar's Tower, was added. After destruction by the Scots in 1388, the keep was uninhabited until it was rebuilt by the indefatigable Lady Anne in 1649-53. Parts of the outer wall date from the 12th century; set into the wall were three round towers, though only one has survived.

Today the castle is in private hands, and is used as a training and conference centre. It also houses the Rare Breeds Survival Trust, which seeks to ensure the survival of endangered animals and birds. The castle and grounds are open to the public from Easter to the end of September. One of the main attractions is a triptych which portrays Lady Anne as a girl of 15 and then at age 54 (when she finally managed to claim her inheritance).

A good view of the castle can be had from Scattergate Green, before you retrace your steps along Shaw's Wiend, and down Doomgate. This street once formed the main road into town from Kendal. A stream ran down the middle of it, from Scattergate to the river, and the horses' hooves would continually be churning up the mud. So the street earned the name "Doemgate", which simply means "the mucky street".

Notice Doomsgate Hall and the old brewery, which is now a fine art and picture framing shop. Soon you come to the junction with High Wiend. These wiends are narrow streets radiating from the market place which, in times of conflict, could be effectively blocked off.

Appleby was designed from the beginning with defence very much in mind. The town was provided with a very effective and natural barrier, being surrounded on three sides by a wide bend in the river Eden, which cut down the directions from which attacks on the town could be mounted. Even the church at the lower end of Boroughgate was fortified.

St Lawrence's is a fine Early English church. The base of the tower is Norman, while the nave dates from the 14th century when Appleby's prosperity was at its peak. Twice the church suffered fire damage, though it was restored in 1654 by Lady Anne Clifford — an event marked by an inscription on one of the roof timbers.

The church organ, too, has had a long and interesting history. Today it dominates the west of the church, but it started out in Carlisle cathedral. The Dean of Carlisle gave it to Appleby in 1684, though it is thought to incorporate parts of an organ which dates back even further, to 1571: a date supported by recent research into original parts of the organ. From 1722, when it was rededicated and brought back into use, until 1863, it stood at the west end of the church. It was then moved to the north aisle, a manoeuvre which necessitated shortening the tower and pipes.

An appeal in 1976 — Architectural Heritage Year — made possible a complete overhaul of the organ. It was re-

The high cross at the head of Appleby's main street, Boroughgate, marked the southern boundary of the market.

stored to its original height and given pride of place once again in the west end of the church. It is recognised as being one of the oldest organs in the country which is still in full use, and its tone, too, is one of the finest.

The church is Lady Anne Clifford's last resting place. She spent many years attempting to claim her rightful inheritance. When she was successful, after nearly 40 years, she occupied herself with travelling between her properties and overseeing their restoration. Her influence can be felt strongly to this day.

She died in 1676, at the ripe old age of 86. Her tomb is in the north aisle of the church, together with a heraldic representation of the Clifford family tree. To the right is the tomb of her mother, which has an effigy of her carved in alabaster.

Outside the church are the handsome cloisters, built on the site of what had been the butter market since 1203. Walk through the cloisters and turn left along Bridge Street. The original Appleby Bridge, of medieval construction, was reckoned to be unsafe by the 1880s, and was replaced by the present bridge in 1889.

Cross the bridge and turn right; the first building on your right was formerly the House of Correction, where prisoners from the gaol were put to work on a treadmill. Across the road is the gaol itself, now the police station. Shire Hall, which housed the Assize Court, was added later in a matching style.

To visit the railway station, walk up the ginnel, past Victorian houses built up on steep terraces. This part of town was only developed with the opening of the Eden Valley Railway in 1862, and the Settle-Carlisle line 14 years later.

Unlike some other ports of call on the Settle-Carlisle line, Appleby's station is no more than a short walk from the town centre. It is now the only manned station between Settle and Carlisle. The station itself is a more substantial version of the "Midland Gothic" buildings to be seen all along the line. In addition to the standard signs, the station name is picked out in white-painted stones on an embankment behind the platform.

A plaque on the station wall commemmorates the Rt Rev Eric Treacy, bishop and keen railway photographer, who collapsed and died at the station in 1978 while waiting to photograph a steam train.

A notice to travellers offers souvenir tickets: "an attractive and nostalgic memento of your visit: traditional card tickets, as invented by Thomas Edmondson".

Just outside the station is a pub called the Midland — a reminder of earlier days and the railway company that built the line.

Make your way back down to Bridge Street. Recross the bridge and turn immediately right along the riverside path to the Butts. Pass the swimming pool and go into Chapel Street, named after the Wesleyan chapel — now just a warehouse — which dates from 1823. The tallest houses in the street comprised Appleby Grammar School from 1604 to 1887, after which the school was moved to new premises on Battlebarrow — the site of one of the shanty towns which housed the navvies who built the Settle-Carlisle railway.

Go left into Low Weind to find yourself back where you started — by the Low Cross in the market place. ❏

Typical of towns and villages in the Eden valley are sturdy sandstone houses, with heavy window surrounds painted in contrasting colours. This is High Wiend in Appleby.

8. Carlisle City Trail

Our tour of the imposing border city — whose castle held out against many Scottish raiding parties — reveals some surprises.

CARLISLE (*Luguvalium* to the Romans, *Caerliwelydd* to the Welsh) has had a long and turbulent history. For 250 years it was a Roman settlement. In the sixth century it formed part of the British kingdom of Rheged, whose rulers Urien and Owain defeated the English at the battle of Argoed Llwyfain. In 685 St Cuthbert was shown round the Roman remains by the governor. In the ninth century the Danes razed it to the ground. In 1066 it was part of Scotland — which explains why it is not mentioned in the Domesday Book. For centuries afterwards it was ravaged in turns by both the English and the Scots. It was besieged as late as 1745, and remained a fortified city into the early years of the last century.

Our tour, which is almost entirely within the old city walls, can be completed in two to three hours if you are in a hurry, though more time would be better.

On emerging from the railway station into Court Square, pause to admire the Tudor-style station frontage, designed in 1847 by Sir William Tite. The porte-cochère you see in front enabled gentlefolk to alight from their carriages and enter the station without getting wet. By 1876 the station served seven different railway companies, of which the Midland was the last to arrive.

The two enormous drum-shaped towers away to your right comprise the Citadel, and mark the southernmost extent of the city walls. The original Citadel (built in 1540, on the orders of Henry VIII) had the towers closer together, with a solid wall between. The actual entrance (the "English Gate") was round the corner, approached by a bridge and with thick wooden gates reinforced with iron. Dilapidated by 1807, that Citadel was demolished (not without protests from conservationists) and rebuilt as Assize Courts.

Cross over the left-hand tower, noting the toll board — a relic of privileges granted to the citizens of Carlisle to ensure their loyalty to the crown of England. Follow the path to the left in front of the tower, past the six-pounder gun and plaque, down to English Damside where the corporation dam and mill-race used to be. The high wall to the right belonged to the county gaol, which was closed in 1922. Turn right along English Damside and right again just before Victoria Viaduct. Go up Bush Brow, then left under a dark bridge to Backhouse Walk. This area of tall, stone warehouses (some several storeys higher on one side than on the other) has a character all its own.

At the end of Backhouse Walk is a fine stretch of the city wall (built 1092-1200 and repaired on and off ever since). The fortified city was about 1,000 yards north-south and a maximum of 400 east-west, with the Castle at the northern tip. This was the West Wall, the East having been demolished in the name of progress at the same time as the Citadel.

Punctuating the wall is Sally Port, one of several small gates used by a besieged army to "sally forth" for a

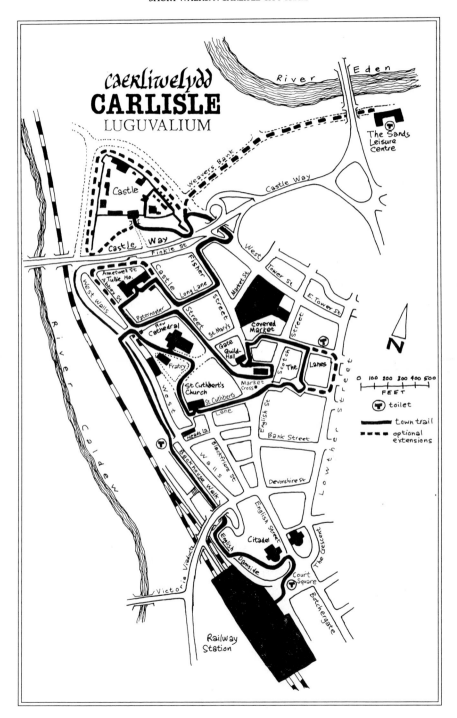

surprise attack, or (more often) to commandeer any edible creature rash enough to stray within reach.

The longest of Carlisle's many sieges was during the Civil War (October 1644 to June 1645); an entertaining eyewitness account by Isaac Tullie can be bought locally. People paying tithes to the Cathedral also had the doubtful privilege of bringing them through this gate, thus avoiding paying tolls.

Follow the path along the foot of the wall. This was completed in 1989, following demolition of the old police station and Fawcett Schools. Plaques from those buildings are preserved in the wall. On reaching a flight of steps, go up, cross the street (appropriately named West Walls) into Dean Tait's Lane. Archibald Tait was Dean of the cathedral from 1850; besides being a great preacher, he organised the restoration by Ewart Christian of the then dilapidated cathedral. In 1856 he became the object of national sympathy when five of his young children died in an epidemic of scarlet fever. Queen Victoria offered him the See of London, and he later became Archbishop of Canterbury.

Turn right through the Cathedral Gatehouse (rebuilt 1527) into the Cathedral Precinct. On the right is the charming Cathedral Registry, dated 1699 and signed "Thomas Carliol". He was Thomas Smith — Dean, historian, antiquarian and later Bishop. Beyond the registry is the Deanery, built on either side of the Prior's Lodging. Until 1540 the cathedral was part of an Augustinian Priory, which was founded about 1102. The Prior's Lodging was built as a pele tower (one of many in the border country) to serve as a lookout and refuge against marauding clans. It is open to the public on request.

Between the Deanery and the cathedral is the Fratry or monks' refectory (early 14th century, remodelled about 1500). Attached to it was the Dormitory;

both were linked to the cathedral by cloisters, of which some remains can be seen. The upper floor of the Fratry now houses the cathedral library, while there is an excellent snack bar and bookshop in the undercroft.

Dominating the scene is the cathedral. It takes about an hour to view it properly, and a full description is beyond the scope of this town trail. There are usually volunteer guides who will be glad to show you round and answer questions (except during service). Ask to see the Genesis Window, Dolphin's Runes, the Brougham Triptych, Prior Senhouse's tomb, the Wall Paintings, the Salkeld Screen, the Misericords, the Prisoners' Graffiti, the Month Capitals, the Deliberate Mistake, and Prior Gondibour's Screen. Other features, such as the Fallen Arches, the Painted Ceiling and the magnificent East Window you can hardly fail to notice for yourself.

For those who have time only to see the outside of the cathedral, the first thing they will notice is that something terrible has happened to the Nave — in fact, most of it has disappeared! After the siege of 1644-5, the victorious Parliamentary commander, General Lesley, had to repair the fortifications in a hurry, and the most convenient source of stone happened to be the nave and cloisters of the Cathedral. The fact that they were already in a dilapidated condition does not excuse that barbaric deed.

To imagine what the nave was like as built by the Normans, look up at the clerestory: the top row of windows. Try to imagine the aisle built in the same stone and the same style, but four times as long as it is now. The south transept is also largely Norman, but the south door dates from the 1850s restoration by Ewart Christian.

Next comes the choir: the east part of the transept. This was completely demolished, then rebuilt longer and wider

A statue of William, Earl of Lonsdale, Lord Lieutenant of Cumberland and Westmorland, stands before the Citadel after which Carlisle's station is named.

145

about 1225. It was badly damaged by fire 70 years later, when a disgruntled disinheritee set fire to the house he had hoped to inherit, and burned most of Carlisle down in the process. The rebuilding of the choir took about 100 years; note the difference in style between the aisles and the clerestory above.

Just before the iron gates, turn right and then, after 50 yards, left to go along the back of the resource centre to St Cuthbert's Church. St Cuthbert himself is said to have founded the first church on this site in 685. Later there was a Norman church, which was demolished in 1778.

The present church dates from 1779, and is typical of its period. Note the tower roof, weather vane, gallery, the record of Sir Walter Scott's marriage, Venetian east window, candelabra, Ferguson memorial, Latvia window and the rail-mounted pulpit. In the churchyard lie buried those who died in the great siege, those executed for supporting Bonny Prince Charlie, felons executed in the gaol, a slave brought back from the West Indies and (it is said) a highwayman.

Walk the length of the church and then straight ahead down St Cuthbert's Lane to the Market Square. The market cross of 1682 is where Bonny Prince Charlie proclaimed his father king in 1745, and many other proclamations have been made there since. The lion on top is holding a representation of the Dormont Book, a code of by-laws drawn up in 1561 which included a curfew on Scottish people.

Continue past the market cross to The Lanes, an award-winning shopping centre opened in 1984. Notice the care that has been taken to make it blend in with its surroundings. It is worth a close inspection, including the loading area at the rear.

Leave the Lanes Centre via Globe Lane, cross Scotch Street and up Rosemary Lane, then turn left into Fisher Street. The building on the right, with overhanging upper storeys, is the 14th century Guildhall. It was restored in 1978 and contains a museum of the trade guilds. After inspecting the front of the Guildhall, turn right (or left if you are coming out of the building), and go down St Alban's Row. Turn right and right again, round to the front of the Old Town Hall — erected in 1717, partly on the site of an Elizabethan building. The cupola was added in 1881. The city council met here until 1964. Notice the mayoral plaques, especially that of Joseph Parker. The Guildhall also houses the Tourist Information Centre.

Carry on towards the Crown and Mitre Hotel, and turn right into Castle Street. The corner house on the right bears a plaque commemorating Sir Walter Scott's marriage. Observe the beautiful flowing tracery of the cathedral east window and, further on, the remains of the nave, where much more Norman work has survived than on the other side.

Turn left into Paternoster Row, right into Georgian Abbey Street, and right again into the grounds of Tullie House — built in 1689 for the Tullie family and one of the most ornate houses in Carlisle. It is now the City Museum, at present undergoing extensive improvements, which are due to be completed in 1991.

On leaving the museum grounds, turn right into Castle Street, noting those houses numbered 26 to 30 (early 18th century with Ionic columns), and number 21 (18th century, handmade bricks).

Immediately before number 21, turn left down Long Lane and left into Fisher Street, noting the working mens' institute opposite: an elegant 19th century house with an unusual serpentine front. Further on is a nine-bay house in chequer brick — once a very fashionable style in Carlisle.

Scant regard for the 'don't lean out of the windows' warning as the Cumbrian Mountain Express steams south out of Carlisle.

At the end of Fisher Street, turn right and right again, then left under the subway into the public park. Looming ahead half-left is the castle, but if in dire need of refreshment, make a short detour via Weaver's Bank and the riverside path to the Sands Leisure Centre self-service restaurant, where you can get anything from a pot of tea to a complete meal every day of the week.

Returning to the castle and note the enormous buttresses supporting the nearest section of wall (the reason for this will be found inside). Walk round the stub of the east city wall and across the lawn towards the outer gatehouse. Carlisle Castle was begun by Henry I of England (on the site of William Rufus's wooden castle) and completed by David of Scotland, who regarded Carlisle as his southern capital. It houses a fascinating museum which tells the history of the castle, and the museum of the King's Own Royal Regiment. It is well worth a visit, but be sure to allow at least an hour, and to arm yourself with the excellent guidebook published by English Heritage.

If you have time on leaving the Castle, you can walk round the outside of the walls. Otherwise, the best way back to the station is via Fisher Street (making a detour to view the handsome covered market), then Market Square and English Street. ❑

10. Clitheroe Town Trail

The revival of regular services on the line which links the Settle-Carlisle route with industrial Lancashire provides the opportunity to explore this interesting historic town.

NOBODY knows exactly how old Clitheroe is. Its name used to be spelt Clyderhow (from Welsh *cludaira*, meaning a heap of stones) and Old Norse (haugr, a small hill), a derivation which suggests considerable antiquity. The town is built on two hills, one occupied by the castle and the other by the parish church. Although containing few buildings of distinction, Clitheroe has many pleasant ones, mostly stone-built, some ashlar-faced, some rendered and painted. It has been described as "half in Lancashire, half in Fairyland".

If you arrive from the south, turn right out of the station and right again under the line to Station Road. The promised resumption of regular services in 1990, comes exactly 140 years after the first train arrived here from Blackburn.

Turn left into King Street, noting the ornate Station Hotel to the right and, on the left, the Old Post House Hotel, whose name and the royal arms at the top proclaim that it was once the post office. Further on you pass Victoria Buildings, a warehouse dating from 1879, and, on the corner at the top, the fine Italianate Barclays Bank.

Turn right into Castle Street, past a couple of pubs on your right — the Swan & Royal, an old coaching inn, and the Starkie Arms, which has a 17th century look about it. Notice the several attractive Victorian shopfronts, notably the opticians on your right.

At the top of the street, cross over and enter the Castle Grounds. Take the path to your left (with panoramic views) up to the Castle Museum. Here, for a small admission fee, you can see and hear exhibits illustrating local history, archaeology, trades, crafts and domestic life. The building dates from the 1740s, and was formerly the Steward's residence.

On leaving the museum, follow the path uphill round to the right, passing the 18th century Court House, left, now housing the north-west sound archives, the site of the Chapel, right, now serving humbler purposes, and the old stables, left, up to the castle keep. Shortly after the Norman Conquest, Orme, the last Saxon Thane of Clyderhow, was evicted from his wooden hall. It was given, along with the lands around it, to Roger de Poitou; he built a stone castle here, but the keep is all that now remains. It last saw action during the Civil War, when the Royalists were besieged for six weeks; they threw all their provisions down the well when they left, to stop them falling into enemy hands. In 1920 the surviving buildings, and its sixteen acres of land, were bought by the Borough of Clitheroe as a war memorial.

Leave the keep by the same steps as you went up. Turn right through the stable arch, then left down the broad track to the Rose Garden, which commemorates the coronation of George VI. The turret in the centre was once part of the Houses of Parliament.

Leave the Rose Garden at the far end, take the steps down to Moor Lane and turn left. On your left is a pleasing for-

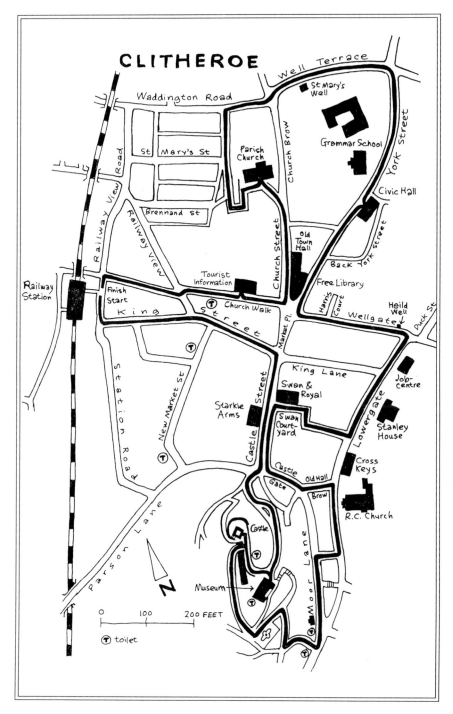

mer school building of 1839, sadly marred by insensitive additions. Cross to the other side of Moor Lane and take the second ginnel on the right (opposite the bookshop) down to Lowergate. Turn left, past St Michael and St John's Roman Catholic Church, built in 1847 by J A Hansom, the inventor of the Hansom Cab. Turn left up Old Hall Brow. It has no sign, but you will recognise it by its attractive surface, paved with setts (sadly tarmaced at the top).

Turn right into Castle Gate, past the United Reformed Church. Go right into Castle Street and right again into Swan Courtyard, which is now an attractive shopping precinct. Continue on down the steps and, before turning left into Lowergate, note the Cross Keys opposite, and a row of windows with "gothic" interlaced glazing bars.

Walk along Lowergate, noting Stanley House (c1720) on the right, and King Lane, left, named after Captain James King, FRS, friend of Captain Cook and navigator on his last voyage. Further on is the former Courthouse (now the Jobcentre) with the royal arms at the top. This crest, and the one on the old post office, would benefit from being painted in their correct colours.

At the crossroads, note Duck Street (roughly opposite) named after the ducking stool which was sited nearby. Turn left into Wellgate and cross over to see Heild Well. Until 1854 Clitheroe depended on this and two other wells for its water supply; there were accusations of extravagance when the waterworks company was finally set up. As you go up Wellgate, note the Victorian and rococo shopfronts on your left, and some vintage advertisements on the wall of Harris Court.

At the top of Wellgate is the Market Place, where the market cross, stocks and pillory once stood. Markets were held here for 900 years until the motor car forced them out. Up to the 17th century Clitheroe was self-sufficient in all produce except iron, salt and tar.

Turn right into York Street, past the studded door of what what once the gaol, to the Civic Hall on the right. If you arrive between 11am and 12.30pm, Monday to Saturday, you should find it open. If not, come back later, because it is not to be missed! From its grand opening in 1874 until the 1920s, all major social events were held here. Later it was run as the Grand Kinema by Ignatius Cullen (who also played the piano). Today it is owned by the Borough Council and operates as a family cinema (the piano is still there). But it is the immaculately maintained interior that makes it an essential part of this town trail.

Next comes Victorian gothic Stanworth House (1781), transferred here stone by stone in 1834 from its original site in the parish churchyard, and then the Royal Grammar School, founded in 1554 by Queen Mary and King Philip. Notable headmasters were William Walbank (1590-1609), accused of frequenting ale-houses and playing bowls in school hours; Abraham Greene (1618-35), accused of beating children "most cruelli"; John Webster, who wrote a book attacking witchcraft in 1677; John Glazebrook (1715-23), tried for murder; Matthew Sedgwick (1750-74), sacked for persistent lateness and absenteeism; and Thomas Wilson (1775-1813), who raised both numbers and standards at the school (apparently not before time). It was amalgamated with the girls' grammar school in 1985.

Turn left into Well Terrace. Here you will find the second of Clitheroe's three wells, St Mary's Well. Go straight across at the roundabout into Waddington Road, and then turn first left into a ginnel or "back" which will bring you to a path and steps leading up to the Parish Church of St Mary Magdalene.

The first known church on this site, built in 1122, was demolished and rebuilt in the early 1400s, only the Norman chancel arch being retained. That second church, which seated fewer than 500 parishioners, was found, by 1828, to be too small. It was replaced by a new one seating 1,150, designed by Thomas Rickman at a cost of £3,500. Only the tower and east window of the 15th century church survived. The Norman chancel arch was carefully taken down and stored, but subsequently went missing. (Bits of it were later found in nearby walls). The spire was added in 1846 and the clerestory in 1898. In May 1979 a fire destroyed the south gallery and south aisle, and badly damaged the organ – all are now repaired at a cost of £300,000. You will find an interesting little guidebook on sale inside the church. Before you leave, read the epitaph on John Robinson's tombstone on the north side of the churchyard. Pause at the west door to admire the view: you should be able to see Longridge Fell, Beacon Fell, Parlick Pike and Totridge Fell.

Leave the church by the short path to Church Street – one of Clitheroe's most attractive thoroughfares. Almost every building is worth a second look. Church Street and Castle Street formed the "backbone" of Clitheroe, linking the three focal points of the castle, market place and church. Near the bottom, on the left, is the old Town Hall, built in 1822 to the designs of Thomas Rickman (an authority on Gothic architecture who also designed the church).

During the local government reorganisation of 1974, Clitheroe lost the borough status that it had held since 1147. The coats of arms, from left to right, are the Cust family, Curzon family, Clitheroe, Lancaster and de Lacy. Next door to the recently refurbished Town Hall is the Free Library, paid for by Andrew Carnegie and completed in 1905 — a most attractive building for its date.

Turn right through the archway into Church Walk and visit the well-stocked Tourist Information Centre. On leaving, continue down the hill, across Railway View and down the ginnel opposite to arrive once again at the railway station. ❏

CARLISLE

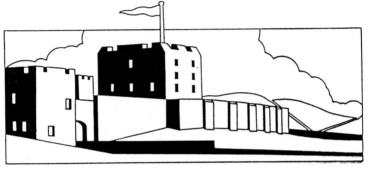

○ *THE GREAT RAILWAY CITY OF THE NORTH*

○ *THE GREAT DAY OUT AT THE END OF THE LINE*

○ *THE GREAT BASE TO TOUR THE BORDERS*

○ *THE GREAT PLACE TO SHOP*

HISTORIC CARLISLE

The Great Border City

Opening times are liable to change without notice, so you may wish to phone and confirm before travelling.

LEEDS-SALTAIRE

LEEDS Tourist Information Centre: 19 Wellington Street. Tel: 0532-462816

Leeds City Art Gallery and Henry Moore Centre, The Headrow. Tel: 0532-462495, open daily.

Leeds City Museum, Calverley Street, Tel 0532- 462465, Open Tues-Sat.

Armley Mills Industrial Museum, Canal Road, Leeds. Tel: 0532-637861.

Kirkstall Abbey, open daily.

Abbey House Museum, Abbey Road, Leeds (next to Kirkstall Abbey). Open weekdays 10-6, Sundays 2-6 (closes at 5pm between October and March). Tel: 0532-755821.

Bradford Industrial Museum, Moorside Road, Greengate, Bradford. Open daily 10-5, closed Mondays (except Bank Holidays) Tel: 0274-631756.

SALTAIRE-SKIPTON

EAST Riddlesden Hall, Bradford Road, Keighley. Open April-November. Tel: 0535-607075.

The Keighley and Worth Valley Railway, Haworth Station, Keighley, West Yorkshire. Tel: general enquiries 0535-45214; talking timetable 0535-43629.

Haworth Tourist Information Centre, 2-4 West Lane. Tel: 0535-42329.

Skipton Castle, open every day ex-

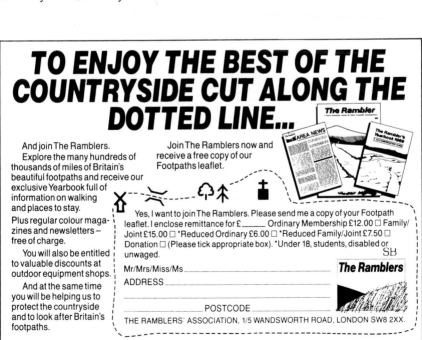

cept Christmas Day, from 10-6 (Sunday 2-6). Tel: 0756-792442.

Embsay Steam Railway, Embsay Station, Nr Skipton. Tel: general enquiries 0756-4727; talking timetable 0756-5189.

Craven Museum, Town Hall, High Street, Skipton. Tel: 0756- 4079.

Skipton Tourist Information Centre, Town Hall Car Park. Tel: 0756-2809.

Boat hire: Pennine Cruisers, The Boat Shop, 19 Coach Street, Skipton. Tel: 0756-5478.

Black Horse Hotel, High Street, Skipton. Tel: 0756-2145.

SKIPTON-SETTLE

SETTLE Tourist Information Centre, Town Hall. Tel: 07292-3877.

Museum of North Craven Life, Victoria Street, Settle. Tel: 0468-61163.

Boat hire: Yorkshire Dales Hire Cruises, Bank Newton, Gargrave, Skipton. Tel: 0756-78492.

SETTLE-RIBBLEHEAD

THE Golden Lion Hotel, Horton-in-Ribblesdale. Tel: 07296-206.

B & B, Mrs J Barker, The Willows, Horton in Ribblesdale. Tel: 07296-373.

Stainforth Youth Hostel. Tel: 07292-3577.

Horton-in-Ribblesdale Tourist Information Centre. Tel: 07296-333.

Station Inn, Ribblehead. Tel: 05242-41274.

RIBBLEHEAD-GARSDALE

Dent Head Youth Hostel. Tel: 05875-251.

Moorcock Inn, Garsdale. Tel: 0969-667488.

GARSDALE-KIRKBY STEPHEN

KIRKBY Stephen Youth Hostel. Tel: 07683-71793.

Kirkby Stephen Tourist Information Centre, Market Place.

The Black Bull Hotel, Kirkby Stephen. Tel: 07683-71237.

Croglin Castle Hotel, South Road, Kirkby Stephen. Tel: 07683-71389.

B &B, Redmayne House, Silver Street, Kirkby Stephen. Tel: 07683-71441.

B & B, Redenol House, 56 South Road, Kirkby Stephen. Tel: 07680-71477.

KIRKBY STEPHEN-APPLEBY

APPLEBY Tourist Information Office, Moot Hall, Boroughgate. Tel: 07683-51177.

Appleby Castle and Rare Breeds Conservation Centre. Open from May-September, daily 10-5. Tel: 07683-51402.

Royal Oak, Bondgate, Appleby. Tel: 07683-51463.

White Hart Hotel, Appleby. Tel: 07683-51598.

B & B, Howgill House, Appleby. Tel: 07683-51574.

APPLEBY-LANGWATHBY

B & B, The Old Vicarage, Edenhall, near Langwathby. Tel: 076881-329.

B & B, Home Farm, Edenhall, near Langwathby. Tel: 076881-203.

B & B, Ashfield, Edenhall, near Langwathby. Tel: 076881-684.

LANGWATHBY-ARMATHWAITE

NUNNERY Walks, near Staffield. Open every day; tearoom open Easter to September.

Dukes Head Hotel, Front Street, Armathwaite. Tel: 06992-226.

B & B, Low Fauld Farm, Ruckcroft, Armathwaite. Tel: 076886-241.

B & B, Vicarage Farmhouse, Armathwaite. Tel: 06992-311.

B & B, Quarry House, Armathwaite. Tel: 06992-282.

ARMATHWAITE-CARLISLE

CARLISLE Tourist Information Centre, The Visitor Centre, Old Town Hall, Greenmarket. Tel: 0228-512444.

Carlisle Castle, open March-September, daily 10-6; October-April, open daily (except Monday) 10-4. Tel: 0228-31777.

SHORT WALKS

BRONTË Parsonage, Haworth, open every day of the year, except December 24, 25 and 26, and from February 1-21. April-Sept 11-5.30; Oct-March 11-4.30. Tel: 0535-42323.

Hawes Youth Hostel. Tel: 0969-667368.

Dales Countryside Museum, Station Yard, Hawes. Tel: 0969-667494. Open April-September, Mon-Sat 11-5, Sunday 2-5.

Hawes Tourist Information Centre. Tel: 0969-667450.

*How long has it been
since you were moved to write great poetry
or paint beautiful pictures?*

*When did you last
glimpse fields of grazing cattle
from the windows of a hurrying train?*

*And when last,
did you course through mountains,
cross rivers and dales?*

*When were you last transported high into the air
to gaze down from majestic viaducts?
Or pause for thought
at England's highest station?*

*And how long is it since you marvelled
at the most breathtaking countryside in all England,
right here on your doorstep?*

*When did you last take the train
from Settle to Carlisle?*

For details of train times and fares
contact your local station or telephone Leeds 448133.

DISCOVER
Britain's
Scenic Railways

Lord Nelson, near Newbiggin, on the royal wedding day, 1981

A series of booklets — entitled Walking East of Eden — is available; for details of these publications (and the Guided Walks programme) send SAE to East Cumbria Countryside Project, Unit 2c, The Old Mill, Warwick Bridge, Carlisle, Cumbria, CA4 8RR.

Join the Friends of the Settle-Carlisle. Membership of FOSCL includes a quarterly newsletter which will keep you informed of news and events concerning the line.

Memberships rates are -

Individual £4.00

Family   £5.00

Corporate £10.00

Enclose SAE with your application, and make cheques/POs payable to FOSCL. Send to Ian Rodham, FOSCL Membership Secretary, 4, Lingwell Crescent, LEEDS LS10 3SZ.

DalesRail guided walks meeting trains from Leeds, Manchester and Preston are held on selected weekends. Leeds programme available from Friends of DalesRail, 3 Rochester Terrace, Leeds LS6 3DF. Tel:0532-759645. Preston programme from Lancashire County Council, Surveyors and Bridgemasters Dept, PO Box 9, Guild House, Cross Street, Preston PR1 8RD. Tel: 0772-263333.

Yorkshire Dales National Park,
Colvend,
Hebden Road,
Grassington,
Skipton,
N Yorkshire BD23 5LB
TEL: 0756-752748

MARKET DAYS

Appleby, Saturday (early closing, Thursday).

Kirkby Stephen: Monday (EC Thursday).

Carlisle: every day except Thursday and Sunday (EC Thursday).

Hawes: Tuesday (EC Wednesday).

Settle: Tuesday (EC Wednesday).

Skipton: Monday, Wednesday, Friday and Saturday (EC Tuesday).

RECOMMENDED READING

Yorkshire Dales National Park, by Tony Waltham, published by Michael Joseph.

The Visitor's Guide to the Yorkshire Dales and North Pennines, by Brian Spencer, published by MPC Ltd.

80 Dales Walks, by Paul Hannon, published by Cordee.

Walks From the Settle-Carlisle Railway, by R W Swallow and W R Mitchell, published by Dalesman.

Great Walks from the Settle & Carlisle, by Colin Speakman and Stan Abbott.

To Kill a Railway, by Stan Abbott, published by Leading Edge Press.

The Line that Refused to Die, by Stan Abbott and Alan Whitehouse, published by Leading Edge Press (summer 1990).

Exploring the Eden Valley, by Gordon Wood, published by Dalesman.

Settle to Carlisle: A Railway Over the Fells, by W R Mitchell and David Joy, published by Dalesman.

The Yorkshire Dales, by Geoffrey White, published by David and Charles.

Through the Carriage Window: Settle & Carlisle, by L Sims and C Darmon, published by Dalesman.

BRITISH RAIL

PASSENGER INFORMATION

Leeds 448133
Bradford 733994
Skipton 2543
Settle 3536
Appleby 51434
Carlisle 44711